# 1000
# House of the Dragon Facts

Scott Ambrose

# Contents


4 - Introduction
5 - 1000 House of the Dragon Facts

111 - photo credit

# INTRODUCTION

Delve deep into the intricate world of Westeros with this comprehensive fact book about the hit prequel series. From the noble houses and their sigils to the blood-soaked battles, dragons, and historical allusions, this book covers everything fans need to know about the epic fantasy saga. Actors, characters, behind the scenes, episodes, influences, dragons, casting, production, differences from the book and so on. All this and much more awaits in 1000 House of the Dragon Facts.

# 1000 HOUSE OF THE DRAGON FACTS

(1) Ten million people watched the House of the Dragon premiere on HBO. This made it the biggest premiere in HBO history.

(2) Milly Alcock said she was washing dishes in a restaurant and living in her mum's attic when she was cast as the young Rhaenyra in House of the Dragon.

(3) The Red Keep was designed to be more open in House of the Dragon than it was in Game of Thrones. This was a deliberate design choice because they wanted the audience to feel this was a place with few secrets where no one could be trusted.

(4) Rhys Ifans, who plays Ser Otto Hightower, was once the lead singer of the pop group Super Furry Animals.

(5) Alicent is nine years older than Rhaenyra in the books but Olivia Cooke is actually a couple of years younger than Emma D'Arcy.

(6) Rhaenyra Targaryen is supposed to be 15 at the start of the show but Milly Alcock was 21 in real life.

(7) The first time we see Ser Criston Cole his armour and weapons are deliberately scruffy and mismatched to indicate that he doesn't come from the most privileged of backgrounds.

(8) Ewan Mitchell said one of his inspirations for Aemond Targaryen was the Halloween movie franchise villain Michael

Myers!

(9) Valyrian steel was inspired by Damascus steel. Damascus steel refers to a type of steel known for its distinctive patterned surface and exceptional properties, making it highly prized for use in knives, swords, and other cutting tools. The term refers to a type of crucible steel produced in the Near East, particularly associated with the city of Damascus in Syria. The steel was known for its ability to be honed to a sharp, resistant edge while having a strong, flexible structure.

(10) The Gothic font used for House of the Dragon was designed by Måns Grebäck. It is influenced by medieval manuscripts.

(11) House of the Dragon production designer Jim Clay had never actually watched Game of Thrones when he was hired on the prequel. He had to binge Game of Thrones to get a feel for the universe the show took place in.

(12) Lead production designer Jim Clay said that when he designed the Red Keep set for House of the Dragon he was inspired by Hilary Mantel's Wolf Hall trilogy about Thomas Cromwell. Clay wanted to try and replicate the Machiavellian aura which made those books so immersive.

(13) Harrenhal is a large castle located in the Riverlands of Westeros. It is considered one of the largest and most formidable castles in the Seven Kingdoms, but it is also known for its dark and cursed history.

(14) Some viewers complained that a beach scene in the episode Driftmark was so dark you couldn't actually see anything. It was even speculated that there had been some

sort of mistake with the 'day for night' shooting (the process where you shoot a scene during the day and darken it to make it look like night). The makers of the show insisted though that the darkness was a deliberate design and mood choice.

(15) Dubrovnik in Croatia not being used as King's Landing in House of the Dragon like it was in Game of Thrones might have had something to do with Dubrovnik struggling to cope with Game of Thrones tourism - to such an extent they began to limit the number of cruise ships which arrived there.

(16) Jamie Kenna, who plays Ser Alfred Broome in House of the Dragon, said he burst into tears when got the part because he was such a big fan of Game of Thrones.

(17) The real location for High Tide on the island of Driftmark was St Michael's Mount. St Michael's Mount is a tidal island in Mount's Bay, Cornwall, England.

(18) The Battle at Rook's Rest was shot in Bourne Wood. Bourne Wood is an area of predominantly coniferous woodland just south of Farnham, Surrey, England. This area has been used in many films.

(19) Olivia Cooke auditioned for the part of Rhaenyra Targaryen before being cast as Alicent Hightower.

(20) The huge dragon skull in the altar of the Red Keep you see in House of the Dragon was actually made from polystyrene.

(21) House of the Dragon is based on George RR Martin's 2018 book Fire & Blood.

(22) Ryan Condal, the showrunner on House of the Dragon,

first met George RR Martin at a book convention in 2005.

(23) We see Rhaenyra eating a lemon cake in season one. This is a little nod to Sansa Stark in Game of Thrones.

(24) Ryan Condal shared showrunning duties with Game of Thrones veteran Miguel Sapochnik on the first season of House of the Dragon. Condal was the solo showrunner for season two.

(25) Sam C. Wilson and Mark Stobbart, who played Blood & Cheese, said the characters were called 'Boris and Charlie' when they did the auditions in order to keep it secret who they were really going to be playing.

(26) For the feast scenes in House of the Dragon, if a character has to eat something they obviously take into account whether the actor is a vegan or vegetarian. In one scene for example a character was eating oysters but in reality they were vegan oysters made with mushrooms.

(27) Renaissance and Byzantine elements influenced the costumes on House of the Dragon.

(28) Matt Smith was a talented footballer as a youngster. He was in the Nottingham Forest youth squad.

(29) House of the Dragon's story (courtesy of George RR Martin's book Fire & Blood) was inspired by 'the Anarchy' - a period of 12th century English history. A civil war was waged between the heirs of King Henry I: his legitimate heir and daughter Matilda and his nephew and closest male heir Stephen of Blois. Rhaenyra Targaryen is based on Matilda.

(30) Emma D'Arcy, who plays Rhaenyra in House of the

Dragon, had never watched Game of Thrones when cast in the prequel.

(31) In the scenes in Game of Thrones where the fugitive Arya Stark is acting as a lowly servant for Tywin, Arya displays a lot of knowledge about Targaryen history.

(32) Fabien Frankel, who plays Ser Criston Cole, is the son of the late actor Mark Frankel. Mark Frankel was born in London in 1962. After a brief career as a professional tennis player, he turned to acting. He was performing in the play Days of Cavafy (above a pub) when he was spotted by casting director Jerry Landon. "One minute I was cycling to the theatre and playing to 40 people," he explained, "the next I was flying to Italy to film the mini-series Michelangelo (in the title role)." He next appeared in another mini-series, Young Catherine, with Julia Ormond and Vanessa Redgrave, and clocked up appearances in such BBC productions as Vanity Dies Hard and Maigret. In 1992 he starred in the well received film Leon the Pig Farmer and in 1994 played a Bondish spy in the short lived television series Fortune Hunter.

Handsome and muscular, Mark Frankel was tested for the part of James Bond in GoldenEye (which was eventually won by Pierce Brosnan) and seemed to have a bright future. Tragically, Mark Frankel, an avid motorcyclist, died in a motorbike accident on the 24th of September 1996.

(33) The production of Game of Thrones was based in Northern Ireland but House of the Dragon is mostly based in England.

(34) The production based for House of the Dragon was Warner Bros. Studios, Leavesden.

(35) Warner Bros. Studios, Leavesden is a studio complex in Leavesden, Hertfordshire, England. The studio used to be an airfield and factory. It was first converted into a studio as a place to make the 1995 Bond film GoldenEye.

(36) Flea Bottom is the slum area of King's Landing. This is where the poor folks live.

(37) The Red Keep set in House of the Dragon was 35,000 square feet in size.

(38) House of the Dragon picks up with the Targaryen dynasty at the height of its power. As we know though, this is not destined to last forever.

(39) In the jousting event you see in the first episode of House of the Dragon, CGI was used to put the faces of actors on the stunt performers.

(40) Paddy Considine said the Iron Throne was very uncomfortable to sit on. He declined to have a cushion because he wanted Viserys Targaryen to look uncomfortable and weary.

(41) Fire & Blood doesn't have as much dialogue as a traditional book so the writers on House of the Dragon had to 'fill in the blanks' (so to speak) more than you would usually have to do in a book to television adaptation.

(42) A dragon will usually only bond with one person.

(43) CGI was used to depict the disfigured face of Viserys I Targaryen later in season one.

(44) The wonderful music in Game of Thrones and House of

the Dragon was by Ramin Djawadi. Djawadi's music is known for its epic and cinematic quality.

(45) 33 gallons of fake blood were used in season two of House of the Dragon.

(46) 144 wigs were used in season two of House of the Dragon.

(47) Moon tea is a medicinal drink to abort a pregnancy. It contains tansy, mint, wormwood, a spoon of honey, and a drop of pennyroyal.

(48) A number of fans and critics were rather perplexed by Matt Smith's character spending a lot of time in season two moping around Harrenhal. It did seem slightly odd to sideline one of your most charismatic cast members this way.

(49) Paddy Considine said he felt a bit envious when season two started shooting because he was obviously not in the show anymore.

(50) Valyrian steel swords are often passed down through generations of noble families as heirlooms and are considered symbols of power and prestige.

(51) The Peak District national park in England has been used for location shooting in House of the Dragon. The green hills and valleys of the Peak District were perfect to depict the Vale.

(52) House of the Dragon has a catering department with huge ovens to prepare food for feast scenes in the show.

(53) The Great Sept of Baelor in King's Landing is yet to be built when Fire & Blood takes place.

(54) The first season of House of the Dragon was complicated by Covid and took longer than expected.

(55) Fabien Frankel initially did a self-taped audition for House of the Dragon but then didn't hear anything for six months. He said he was surprised to get the part because he didn't think his taped audition was very good.

(56) King's Landing was usually depicted as a very sunny and hot place in Game of Thrones but it often looks quite bleak in House of the Dragon.

(57) You can buy a House of the Dragon themed fire breathing dragon lamp.

(58) House of the Dragon has used as many as 250 extras for battle scenes.

(59) Rhaenyra is more sympathetic in the television show than she is in the book.

(60) The change from ten episodes to eight for season two was apparently made by HBO only a month before shooting and so required some changes to the end of the season.

(61) The showrunner and producers on House of the Dragon said that season two only having eight episodes had nothing to do with them and was a decision they had no control over.

(62) Valyrian steel, though much stronger, is lighter than normal steel.

(63) Season two of House of the Dragon took 270 days to shoot.

(64) The dry dock at Driftmark was constructed in the backlot at Leavesden.

(65) Clips from the season two finale of House of the Dragon were illegally uploaded to TikTok weeks before the episode was aired.

(66) Ewan Mitchell said he doesn't believe House of the Dragon is ever violent purely for the sake of being violent,.

(67) Fabien Frankel said his costume was so constrictive in season one that he could barely feed himself at lunch.

(68) Paddy Considine was given the freedom to craft and portray King Viserys in his own way.

(69) George RR Martin said that if he was in charge of King's Landing the first he would do would be to improve the sanitation and drains!

(70) The very early working title for House of the Dragon was The Dance of the Dragons.

(71) A scene of Cregan Stark leading his army on the march was cut from the season two finale.

(72) Princess Rhaenys Targaryen is known as the 'Queen who never was' because she was passed over for the Iron Throne due to her gender.

(73) Paddy Considine said he based Viserys I Targaryen on his mother and father - who were very ill at the end of their lives.

(74) Some the cast said the Red Keep set at Leavesden Studios was so huge and impressive that they sometimes wondered if

it would have been cheaper just to buy a real castle!

(75) George RR Martin has complained about the Targaryen dragon sigil in House of the Dragon having four legs instead of two.

(76) The Kingsguard are basically highly skilled knights who act as bodyguards for the royal family. They take a vow of chastity and wear white cloaks.

(77) Mikkeller launched two House of The Dragon themed ales in 2022. The beers were named Syrax and Caraxes. The Caraxes beer was non-alcoholic.

(78) Daemon Targaryen's Valyrian steel sword is called Dark Sister.

(79) One thing that gave HBO confidence with House of the Dragon was that even in 2022 Game of Thrones was still one of their top ten most streamed shows. HBO knew there was still an appetite for productions set in the world created by George RR Martin.

(80) Emily Carey, who played the young Alicent Hightower in season one, has played both the young Lara Croft and the young Diana Prince (Wonder Woman) in movies.

(81) Miguel Sapochnik was a Game of Thrones veteran - having directed acclaimed episodes like Battle of the Bastards and The Winds of Winter.

(82) In a Boston.com poll, 33% of people said they thought House of the Dragon was a 'bit' worse of Game of Thrones and 10% of people said they thought it was a 'lot' worse than Game of Thrones.

(83) The Daily Beast once devoted an article to complaining how bad the wigs were in House of The Dragon. The article said that Lord Corlys looked like Forest Whitaker in Battlefield Earth!

(84) Miguel Sapochnik said that swords from The Witcher and the film Warcraft were used in the Iron Throne for House of the Dragon. This was a consequence of them struggling to find enough swords.

(85) Some fans were disappointed that the Battle of the Gullet did not appear in season two of House of the Dragon. This battle was held back for season three.

(86) House of the Dragon has a user score of 5.3 on Metacritic. This score is described by the site as 'mixed to average'.

(87) Corlys Velaryon is known as the Sea Snake.

(88) Season one of House of the Dragon covers 20 years of history.

(89) Matt Smith said he thinks that, beneath the harsh exterior, Daemon is quite a fragile and vulnerable person.

(90) Mysaria's bizarre accent, according to the actress Sonoya Mizuno, was due to it being changed through ADR. Sonoya said she was later allowed to rectify the accent.

(91) Esquire described House of the Dragon as like The Crown - only with dragons.

(92) Suits of armour in the show are actually made of light plastic.

(93) For a time, House of the Dragon was the most watched HBO show since Game of Thrones. The Last of Us managed to overtake House of the Dragon though to win this accolade.

(94) Food is a symbol of power in House of the Dragon. A huge feast is a way to highlight one's wealth.

(95) House of the Dragon was something of a gamble for HBO because they knew it would be an expensive and there was no guarantee that the show would enjoy anything like the success of Game of Thrones. Thus far though the gamble seems to be paying off reasonably well.

(96) Murray's Bagels in New York produced a line of black and green bagels to celebrate season two of House of the Dragon.

(97) The first season of House of the Dragon wrapped shooting in February 2022.

(98) The shoulders on the costumes of King Viserys I Targaryen went from square to round as the first season progressed to indicate his physical decline and 'slumping' posture.

(99) The set for the Red Keep was built like a real castle that you could walk around. This allowed for characters to have 'real time journeys' walking from room to room.

(100) Targaryens traditionally have black armour.

(101) Matt Smith said he missed Paddy Considine when they started making season two.

(102) You can buy House of the Dragon hoodies and sweatshirts.

(103) George RR Martin said the perfect king in the universe he created would be someone who sees the position as one of duty rather than something he is entitled to.

(104) Olivia Cooke said that when she finishes a hard day's filming on House of the Dragon her first priority is to find a pub!

(105) Milly Alcock said she had never watched Game of Thrones when she was cast in House of the Dragon.

(106) Tom Glynn-Carney might seem familiar as Aegon Targaryen because you probably saw him in Christopher Nolan's Dunkirk. He was the older son on the little boat helping rescue soldiers.

(107) The season two finale of House of the Dragon drew 8.9 million viewers on HBO Max.

(108) HBO gave the green light for House of the Dragon to become a series in October 2019.

(109) House of the Dragon was the first project to be shot at Warner Bros. Leavesden Studios' new virtual production stage.

(110) Ryan Condal described the core theme of House of the Dragon as generational conflict. The arrival of children and new generations simply adds to the feuding and scheming.

(111) Matt Smith asked for his character Daemon to have a belt so that he would have somewhere to 'anchor' his hands in scenes.

(112) There are unavoidably changes from the book in any

television adaptation and House of the Dragon is no exception. Some fans have complained that the events of the book are being rattled through too quickly in the show while others feel they are being dragged out too much. It is impossible to please everyone.

(113) Matt Smith said he thinks that Daemon would be a really terrible king.

(114) House of the Dragon is somewhat atypical for HBO because they tend to go for original shows rather than franchises.

(115) George RR Martin is said to have sold around 90 million books in his career.

(116) In the world of House of The Dragon, having dragons is sort of like having nuclear weapons.

(117) Ravens are the carrier pigeons of the Game of Thrones world and used to send long distance messages.

(118) Game of Thrones star Emilia Clarke said in an interview that she wouldn't be watching House of the Dragon. Emilia said watching the show would be like 'going to someone else's school reunion'.

(119) House of the Dragon earned 1.23 billion minutes of viewing on HBO Max in the week after its second season premiere.

(120) Jefferson Hall, who plays twins Jason Lannister and Tyland Lannister in House of the Dragon, appeared in two episodes of Game of Thrones as Ser Hugh of the Vale.

(121) Season one House of the Dragon costume designer Jany Temime had never actually seen Game of Thrones when she was hired on the prequel.

(122) There were 400 different costumes created for the main cast in season two of House of the Dragon.

(123) George RR Martin seemed to do less blog posts about season two of House of the Dragon compared to his effusive praise for season one.

(124) Millie Alcock said that when she did her tape audition for the show she had no idea at first that it was a Game of Thrones spin-off. All she knew initially is that she was auditioning for an 'unamed HBO' project.

(125) Fire & Blood is designed to read like a slightly unreliable history.

(126) Ewan Mitchell said that Peter O'Toole's Lawrence of Arabia was another one of his inspirations for Aemond Targaryen.

(127) Caroline McCall took over as the costume designer in season two. A lot of the costumes were modified in season two to symbolise the houses drifting apart.

(128) Ryan Condal said in 2024 that House of the Dragon will run to four seasons.

(129) You can buy House of the Dragon fridge magnets.

(130) The Hand of the King is the king's most senior and high ranking advisor. This is a very powerful position to hold because of the influence you have over the ruler.

(131) House of The Dragon star Matt Smith said he was always a big Game of Thrones fan. He said he actually met George RR Martin at a comic con before Game of Thrones had even come out on television.

(132) Freddie Fox, who plays Gwayne Hightower, is another member of the Fox family acting dynasty. He is the son of Edward Fox.

(133) The Triarchy is the name given to the alliance between the Free Cities of Lys, Myr and Tyros.

(134) House of the Dragon went into production around the same time as Amazon's expensive Lord of the Rings show The Lord of the Rings: The Rings of Power. House of the Dragon, by most metrics, proved to be more successful though than the Lord of the Rings show.

(135) The Lord of the Rings: The Rings of Power cost $450 million more than House of the Dragon.

(136) The cast had to have regular Covid tests when they shot season one.

(137) The crown worn by King Viserys I Targaryen in the show was really lightweight resin painted to look like metal.

(138) The ale drunk in the show is really just coloured water.

(139) Monsanto in Portugal was one of the places used to depict the exteriors of Dragonstone.

(140) Gold Cloaks are the City Watch of King's Landing. Their duties are to defend the city and maintain law and order.

(141) HBO said they started knocking around ideas for a Game of Thrones spin-off a few years before Game of Thrones came to an end.

(142) Phil Daniels, who plays Maester Gerardys in House of the Dragon, has done many things but will probably always be best known for lead performance in the cult film Quadrophenia.

(143) Fabien Frankel said that during breaks in filming he has to be 'ventilated' because his armpits get smelly wearing all that armour!

(144) Paddy Considine said he wanted to take home his character's dagger as a memento but HBO are not too keen on giving props away.

(145) House of the Dragon's first season got a little bit of criticism for rushing through the story too quickly whereas with season two some felt it moved through the story too slowly.

(146) Ewan Mitchell said that Kirk Douglas in Vikings was another one of his inspirations for Aemond Targaryen.

(147) Fabien Frankel was in a film with Game of Thrones star Emilia Clarke called Last Christmas. Sadly for Fabien though a lot of his scenes ended up on the cutting room floor.

(149) Dragons are often associated with the elements of fire and water, symbolizing destruction and creation.

(150) Ty Tennant is only nine years younger than Olivia Cooke despite playing her son in the show.

(151) You can buy chocolate dragon eggs from online candy stores.

(152) Ewan Mitchell, who plays Aemond Targaryen, is no stranger to popular historical epics because he played Osferth in The Last Kingdom.

(153) Matt Smith said that one of the things which persuaded him to do House of the Dragon was that he's always wanted to work with Paddy Considine.

(154) Milly Alcock as Rhaenyra Targaryen is generally held up as having the best wig on the show.

(155) The dragon Caraxes is known as the Blood Wyrm.

(156) Matt Smith's career stuttered a bit after he left Doctor Who (his scenes in a Terminator sequel famously hit the cutting room floor) but thanks to The Crown and House of the Dragon he seems to be going from strength to strength.

(157) The Accursed Kings series by Maurice Druon was an influence on George RR Martin's books. The Accursed Kings is a historical fiction series set in medieval France during the reign of King Philip IV. The series follows the power struggles, betrayals, and political intrigue of the French royal court, as various factions vie for control of the throne.

(158) The dragon Vhagar is named after the old Valyrian God of War.

(159) You can buy House of the Dragon cushions.

(160) Dance of the Dragons is the term for the Targaryen civil war.

(161) Despite the Screen Actors Guild (SAG) strikes in 2023, House of the Dragon was one of the big American shows that was able to carry on shooting because it was made in Britain under contracts through the British actors union Equity. House of the Dragon was fortunate too that the scripts were already completed so this meant no one violated the writer's strike.

(162) For the dragon riding scenes in House of the Dragon, the actors in the mechanical bull type contraption have to endure wind machines and water being thrown at them. Matt Smith said it does get a bit exhausting in the end.

(163) It took ten months to shoot the first season of House of the Dragon.

(164) House of the Dragon hair designer Rosalia Culora said some of the wigs in the show cost 'five figures' to make.

(165) Matt Smith said he actually did a re-watch of Game of Thrones in preparation for House of the Dragon.

(166) You can buy an Aegon Targaryen House of the Dragon Soy Wax Candle. The candle's scent is cedar and 'sea notes'.

(167) Though it was probably unavoidable due to the time jump, some viewers felt it was a shame Milly Alcock was only in part of season one because her performance was one of the highlights.

(168) Emma D'Arcy is nonbinary. Emma said it isn't a big deal and can be a bit 'boring' to have to explain or talk about.

(169) Syrax is the first dragon to appear in House of the Dragon.

(170) Syrax belongs to Rhaenyra.

(171) Rhaenyra and Alicent discuss the legend of Princess Nymeria in season one of House of the Dragon.

(172) Nymeria is the name of Arya Stark's direwolf in Game of Thrones.

(173) There have been some House of the Dragon Funko Pops.

(174) Fabien Frankel said he was terrible in school plays when he was a kid.

(175) The second season premiere of House of the Dragon had 22% less viewers than the first season premiere.

(176) The land north of the wall is a vast area bigger than the United States.

(177) Matt Smith is said to have turned down some big roles in the past because he didn't think they were a good fit for him. He is selective in the work he takes and not one of those actors who does anything he is offered.

(178) Steve Toussaint, who plays Corlys Velaryon in House of the Dragon, said he auditioned for a couple of parts in Game of Thrones but didn't get cast.

(179) Ryan Condal did concede in an interview that season one of House of the Dragon had lighting that was too dark at times. He said he changed this for season two.

(180) It's hard to find any part of the world that does not feature dragons in its ancient folklore or legends.`

(181) Viserys is the firstborn son of Prince Baelon Targaryen and his sister-wife Princess Alyssa Targaryen.

(182) Ewan Mitchell said one of his other inspirations for Aemond Targaryen was Neil McCauley. Neil McCauley is the character played by Robert De Niro in the Michael Mann film Heat. McCauley is a highly professional and unemotional career criminal who stages bank heists. McCauley's code is that you should never form attachments you aren't willing to immediately walk away from if self-preservation dictates.

(183) Fire & Blood is certainly not an easy book to adapt because it is written in the style of a historical essay.

(184) Milly Alcock, who played Rhaenyra Targaryen in the first season of House of the Dragon, was only ten years old when Game of Thrones begun.

(185) Gavin Spokes, who played Lord Lyonel Strong, said when he was cast in House of the Dragon he wasn't allowed to tell anyone for six months because HBO wanted complete secrecy about the project.

(186) The dragon Vhagar is meant to be 103 years old.

(187) HBO were pretty shrewd in putting House of the Dragon on their main channel in the old 9pm Game of Thrones Sunday night slot. This marked something of a return to the days when a lot of people would all sit down and watch something at the same time - a phenomenon that is increasingly rare in our streaming binge at a time of your own choosing age.

(188) Some fans of House of the Dragon think the Red Keep stairs are sometimes used a bit too much in the show!

(189) You can now buy House of the Dragon Monopoly.

(190) When we see mud being thrown over Ser Arryk and Erryk for their burial the two actors were actually having crushed up chocolate cake being thrown over them. They said it was actually quite pleasant!

(191) Miguel Sapochnik said the Iron Throne in House of the Dragon was quite dangerous because it contained some real swords. It was fenced off when not being used for filming.

(192) Monsanto in Portugal was used for some of the Dragonstone exteriors.

(193) Ryan Condal, the showrunner on House of the Dragon, likened having to follow Game of Thrones to a band having to go onstage after The Beatles.

(194) The dragon sequences in the show are mapped out with storyboards and animation before they actually do the dragon special effects.

(195) You can buy a Alicent Hightower Soy Candle & Wax Melt. The candle's scent is pear and freesia.

(196) Emma D'Arcy said they quite enjoyed learning High Valyrian for certain scenes in House of the Dragon.

(197) It is probably fair to say that some fans were disappointed that the season two finale didn't really feel like a finale.

(198) Emily Carey said that when she watched Game of Thrones to prepare for playing Alicent, the violence and nudity was a bit frightening because it made her wonder what

on earth she was going to have to do in the prequel!

(199) Paddy Considine said that while shooting the painful struggle of the ailing Viserys Targaryen to reach the Iron Throne in season one he ended up injuring his hip!

(200) Tom Taylor, who plays Cregan Stark in house of the Dragon, once played the young version of Uhtred in The Last Kingdom. The Last Kingdom is a historical action/adventure show that was sometimes compared to Game of Thrones.

(201) Lesley-Ann Brandt said she auditioned to play (the older) Alicent Hightower. Lesley-Ann Brandt is actually a decade older than Olivia Cooke.

(202) The welcome feast for Rhaenyra and Laenor in season one required 300 costumes to be made for the cast and extras.

(203) Emily Carey was seventeen when she played Alicent in season one.

(204) Castles are fortified strongholds built to protect against enemy attacks and to assert control over the surrounding land.

(205) Ryan Condal said that season two of House of the Dragon is about the 'fits and starts' of war whereas season three will be total war.

(206) Season two of House of the Dragon has a new opening title sequence depicting a tapestry of Targaryen history.

(207) According to HBO about 30% of House of the Dragon's audience comes from cable.

(208) Olivia Cooke said that some scenes on House of the Dragon can take two weeks to film.

(209) HBO said they never worried about House of the Dragon overlapping or going up against Amazon's Rings of Power. They said they just concentrated on their own show and didn't worry about what others were doing.

(210) House of the Dragon is obviously a slightly different experience for those familiar with George RR Martin's books because those people will notice what was changed and what was left out more than casual viewers.

(211) Valyrian steel has a rippled effect like water.

(212) Emma D'Arcy did their initial House of the Dragon audition on an iPhone.

(213) Matt Smith said he has taken home a prop of Daemon's sword Dark Sister and keeps it in his kitchen.

(214) House of the Dragon has been described as a 'slow burn' type of show. It doesn't throw in action and battles for the sake of it.

(215) High Tide is the seat of House Velaryon.

(216) Steve Toussaint, who plays Corlys Velaryon in House of the Dragon, said he deliberately avoided reading the book because he knew it would differ from the scripts somewhat and he wanted to base his performance strictly on the scripts.

(217) You can buy Aemond Targaryen Fragrance on Etsy. The smell is described as spicy, leathery, and citrusy.

(218) King Viserys I Targaryen was the last rider of the dragon Balerion. Balerion was known as Black Dread.

(219) Emma D'Arcy and Olivia Cooke said the first scene they shot together was a funeral scene for episode seven of season one.

(220) You can now buy House of the Dragon playing cards.

(221) The marketing campaign for season one of House of the Dragon was the largest HBO had ever undertaken at the time.

(222) The first recorded dragon story is from ancient Sumeria, dating back to around 2000 BC.

(223) North Wales was used for some of the Vale scenes in season two of House of the Dragon.

(224) Matt Smith got a slight head injury shooting the early scene where Ser Criston spars with Prince Daemon Targaryen. It was nothing too serious.

(225) House of the Dragon takes place 172 years prior to the birth of Daenerys.

(226) Some people dubbed House of the Dragon a 'Medieval Call the Midwife' in season one because of all the birth scenes!

(227) Olivia Cooke said the whole point of House of the Dragon is that the viewer is supposed to be conflicted over which side they are on - to the point where they don't really want to pick any side.

(228) House of the Dragon is not shot chronologically - which can be a bit confusing at the times for the actors.

(229) Seven Kingdoms Cellars, of Vintage Wine Estates, worked with Warner Bros. and HBO to launch some House of the Dragon wines in 2022. The wines were a California cabernet sauvignon, a blended red from the Lodi appellation in California, and a 2021 Oregon pinot noir.

(230) King Viserys I Targaryen is the great-great-great-great-great-grandfather of King Aerys II Targaryen (aka The Mad King).

(231) The promotional budget for the second season of House of the Dragon was said to be $100 million.

(232) Warner Bros. Studios, Leavesden was also used for the Harry Potter films.

(233) The second season of House of the Dragon got the green light only days after the first season premiere.

(234) House of the Dragon has a long way to go to match the record viewership for a single episode of Game of Thrones - which stands at 19.3 million.

(235) Matt Smith portrayed Prince Philip (the Duke of Edinburgh) in The Crown. Prince Philip was the husband of Queen Elizabeth II.

(236) One of the problems House of the Dragon has faced is that the dragon special effects eat up a chunk of the budget.

(237) Voters on the Ranker website have Prince Daemon Targaryen as the best character in the show.

(238) Emmy D'Arcy did not watch any of Milly Alcock's scenes before taking over as Princess Rhaenyra Targaryen because

the producers wanted Emmy's performance to be its own thing and not some sort of imitation.

(239) Fabien Frankel said, to his great relief, they made Ser Criston Cole's armour costume lighter to wear in season two.

(240) House of the Dragon was an important project for HBO because it was the first time they had tested the waters to see if Thrones spin-offs were viable.

(241) The cast on House of the Dragon have to work six days a week to get a season in the can.

(242) Emma D'Arcy said it is quite commonplace to work fifteen hour days on House of the Dragon.

(243) There is a 'House of the Dragon/Game of Thrones - Seat of Power Board Game' you can buy online.

(244) King Viserys I is the fifth Targaryen ruler.

(245) Fire & Blood and follows the Targaryen family, focusing on the events leading up to the civil war known as the Dance of the Dragons.

(246) George RR Martin described House of the Dragon as being like a Shakespearean tragedy.

(247) Emma D'Arcy read Fire & Blood in preparation for House of the Dragon.

(248) Joffrey talks about the fate of Rhaenyra Targaryen in a Game of Thrones scene. In hindsight, this is actually a spoiler for House of the Dragon!

(249) Fabien Frankel said he was a huge Game of Thrones fan - to the point where it was quite daunting to be cast in a prequel.

(250) Ramin Djawadi created the iconic theme song in just a few days.

(251) A full sized dragon is 230 feet long.

(252) House of the Dragon is shown on Sky Atlantic in much of Europe.

(253) In what was seen as a slightly surprising move, the Game of Thrones theme music is also used for the titles in House of the Dragon.

(254) The linguist David J. Peterson created the fictional languages used in Game of Thrones and House of the Dragon.

(255) Daemon Targaryen's dragon is called Caraxes.

(256) After the end of Game of Thrones, its showrunners Dan Weiss and David Benioff were offered a lucrative contract where they would have a producer credit on all prequels and spin-offs. They turned this down though because they were not comfortable with the idea of getting paid for a show they had little to do with.

(257) The first season finale of House of the Dragon leaked to torrent sites before it was on HBO. HBO blamed a foreign broadcast partner for the leak.

(258) Olivia Cooke had done many things before House of the Dragon but she was best known for her role as Emma Decody in the popular television show Bates Motel.

(259) Ser Criston Cole originates from the Dornish Marches.

(260) Before the development of House of the Dragon, HBO did a pilot for a prequel show called Bloodmoon. The pilot's cast included Naomi Watts and Jamie Campbell Bower and was set 1,000 years before Game of Thrones. The story was allegedly about the first conflict with the White Walkers and the building of the Wall.

(261) HBO spent $30 million on the Bloodmoon pilot but decided not to go ahead with a series. The pilot has never been seen.

(262) HBO said the Bloodmoon pilot did not 'gel' and felt it wasn't strong enough to be a show. It was written by Jane Goldman and an original story not based on any books.

(263) Bloodman was designed to be very different to Game of Thrones and was described as very ambitious. In the end though HBO obviously got cold feet and decided to pivot away to the slow burn political intrigue of House of the Dragon.

(264) Other notable actors who appeared in the aborted Bloodmoon prequel were Miranda Richardson, John Simm, and Narnia star Georgie Henley.

(265) The Bloodmoon pilot was directed by S. J. Clarkson. Clarkson said the pilot was great and said she had no idea why HBO abandoned the project. Clarkson is a prolific television director but sadly is best known now as the director of the infamous megabomb film Madame Web.

(266) HBO did extensive promotion for the second season of House of the Dragon which included digital promos and banners at the Empire State Building.

(267) Marketing analysts said that HBO's promotion for season one of House of the Dragon 'reached' 130 million Americans.

(268) Matt Smith said that any fan grumbling about his casting in House of the Dragon didn't bother him too much because he experienced something similar when he was initially cast as the Doctor in Doctor Who. He said you just have to shut out all the outside noise and focus on your performance.

(269) Kit Harington has always been keen to do a Jon Snow spin-off show which would potentially feature other characters from Game of Thrones. Sadly though, in 2024 he said the project had been put on ice indefinitely because they couldn't decide what the story should be. HBO seem more interested in Game of Thrones prequels than a Jon Snow spin-off show.

(270) In 2019 it was estimated that HBO had made at least a couple of billion from Game of Thrones merchandise. House of the Dragon has doubtless added to that number.

(271) You can buy House of the Dragon water bottles.

(272) When the show began, George RR Martin said he had more creative input on House of the Dragon than he did on Game of Thrones. It seems to be case though that his influence evaporated on season two.

(273) Paddy Considine said he never watched Game of Thrones when it was on but did start watching it during the lockdowns. He said he was about half-way through when he was offered House of the Dragon - which he found a weird coincidence.

(274) Emma D'Arcy is brunette in real life.

(275) George RR Martin said they considered (like the book) having a framing sequence in House of the Dragon where the Archmaester is narrating this tale to us from years in the future. In the end they decided not to do this.

(276) You can buy a Helaena Targaryen House of the Dragon Soy Wax Candle. The scent notes are vanilla, sea salt, and caramel.

(277) House of the Dragon picks up after the cold open nine years into Viserys's reign.

(278) The second season only having eight episodes was something that irritated fans.

(279) Daemon Targaryen is known as the Rogue Prince.

(280) HBO were attracted to George RR Martin's books because they correctly deduced they could have world wide appeal with the medieval/fantasy aura.

(281) Caesar's Camp was a shooting location season one of House of the Dragon. Caesar's Camp is an Iron Age hill fort straddling the border of the counties of Surrey and Hampshire in southern England.

(282) Daemon Targaryen has a Valyrian steel helmet in the show. This was not the case in the books.

(283) House of the Dragon is smaller in scope than Game of Thrones because it has a tighter focus on a specific conflict

(284) Paddy Considine said he was told right from the start

that he would only be in the first season.

(285) The cremation in season one where Rhaenyra has Syrax light the pyre was shot at St Catherine's Tor near Hartland Quay in Devon.

(286) After the second season finished and House of the Dragon took a break, HBO moved the series Industry into its time slot. By a quirk of coincidence, Game of Thrones star Kit Harington had just joined the cast of Industry.

(287) The Driftmark set with the ship in the harbour took about sixteen weeks to build.

(288) Paddy Considine said he was delighted to briefly reprise his role in House of the Dragon for dream sequences in season two.

(289) Targaryens have purple eyes in the books. The reason they didn't do this in the television shows goes back to the start of Game of Thrones and Emilia Clarke finding it too difficult to wear contact lenses for her scenes.

(290) Salisbury Plain has been used for filming in House of the Dragon. Salisbury Plain is a large chalk plateau in Wiltshire. Part of the plain is owned by the British Army and used for military training exercises.

(291) Milly Alcock's real name is Amelia May Alcock.

(292) Director of photography Catherine Goldschmidt said she enjoyed staging the Harrenhal scenes in season two because it was a bit like working on a haunted house horror film.

(293) Scenes of the wedding between Alicent Hightower and

King Viserys were shot but cut from the show because there wasn't room for them.

(294) Sir Arryk and Sir Erryk are played by twins Luke and Elliott Tittensor.

(295) Paddy Considine said there were some obvious influences like Phantom of the Opera, Hunchback of Notre Dame, and the Elephant Man for when King Viserys I Targaryen is disfigured and has to wear a mask.

(296) The first season of House of the Dragon had premieres in Amsterdam, Mexico City, Los Angeles, and London.

(297) At the season two House of the Dragon premiere in New York there was (appropriately enough) a green carpet rather than a red carpet.

(298) Matt Smith wore an Armani suit to the London premiere of season two.

(299) Olivia Cooke was in the Steven Spielberg film Ready Player One. It wasn't really one of Spielberg's best.

(300) Emily Carey (who played the young Alicent) said she only got to see Olivia Cooke as Alicent when House of the Dragon came out. She wasn't afforded a sneak peak.

(301) Emma D'Arcy and Olivia Cooke had already started shooting when Emily Carey and Milly Alcock first arrived on the set to play the younger versions of their characters.

(302) George RR Martin turned down a cameo in Game of Thrones because he didn't want to fly all the way to Belfast. He did though sort of make a cameo in House of the Dragon

because the weirwood tree was made to resemble him.

(303) George RR Martin did have a cameo in the (largely) unseen Game of Thrones pilot but his scene (like so much of that original pilot) has never been shown. He was a guest at a wedding in the pilot.

(304) In the lore, there are only a limited number of Valyrian steel items left in the world, making them valuable and rare.

(305) You can buy House of the Dragon sunglasses.

(306) Emily Carey said it was a great acting education for her to work with Paddy Considine.

(307) Daemon is pretty harsh when it comes to law and order. He has thieves lose their hands.

(308) Vaemond Velaryon is the nephew of Corlys in the book.

(309) Game of Thrones would usually (though not always) start in March. Some fans thought it was a slightly strange decision to put season two of House of the Dragon on in the summer - a time when people tend to go out more and watch less television.

(310) For the Harrenhal interiors in House of the Dragon, they built a set for the throne section and then used CG effects for the rest of the castle.

(311) The members of the Small Council in House of the Dragon have a stone on a sort of marble plate in front of them. Ryan Condal said the stones are essentially like punching a clock to signal someone has turned up for work.

(312) George RR Martin said on his blog that he thinks Rhys Ifans has made a 'splendid' Otto Hightower.

(313) Ryan Condal was working on a Conan the Barbarian adaptation for Amazon just before he got House of the Dragon. The Conan project was axed - which allowed Condal to move to HBO.

(314) When she was very young, Olivia Cooke auditioned for the British soap opera Emmerdale but got rejected.

(315) The first name of Rhys Ifans is pronounced as 'Reese'.

(316) Laena Velaryon dies in childbirth in the book. The suicide by dragon moment is an invention of the television show.

(317) You can buy House of the Dragon enamel pins.

(318) Larys Strong is known as The Clubfoot.

(319) Olivia Cooke said she toned down her strong northern English accent to help her acting career. Olivia is from Greater Manchester in Lancashire.

(320) Matt Smith kept hold of the tweed jacket he wore when he played the Doctor in Doctor Who.

(321) When he was a young unknown aspiring actor, Matt Smith unsuccessfully tested for the part of Will McKenzie in the cult British comedy show The Inbetweeners. It was Simon Bird who won this part in the end.

(322) In the book, Alicent is present for the Blood and Cheese scene. In the television show she isn't.

(323) Filming on House of the Dragon actually started in the year that HBO were celebrating the tenth anniversary of Game of Thrones.

(324) George RR Martin said he likes his stories to evolve naturally as part of the writing process and doesn't plan every detail in advance.

(325) The Anarchy, on which the story in House of the Dragon is based, ended in 1153 with the Treaty of Wallingford, in which it was agreed that Matilda's son, Henry II, would succeed Stephen as king.

(326) Matt Smith's full name is Matthew Robert Smith.

(327) A section of House of the Dragon fans get very irritated when the show changes something from the book. It is obviously very difficult to adapt a book with a strong cult following and keep everyone happy.

(328) One of the main reasons why the spin-off show Bloodmoon was axed after a (unbroadcast) pilot is that the period of history it depicted was one that George RR Martin had only written a few lines about. This meant that the Bloodmoon writers would have to make it all up themselves. While this isn't necessarily an impossible obstacle it does seem as if HBO decided in the end they'd rather do something that had a slightly more substantial Martin text to follow and borrow from.

(329) In 2019, Fabien Frankel played Theo Sipowicz (the son of the Dennis Franz character) in an attempted reboot of the classic police show NYPD Blue. However, the pilot was not deemed strong enough to go to a series and the project was axed. Had the show gone ahead Fabien would not have been

available for House of the Dragon.

(330) You can buy the first season soundtrack of House of the Dragon on vinyl.

(331) You can buy a House of the Dragon cookie jar online.

(332) A giant inflatable 'air wall' was put around the Leavesden studio backlot in 2021 to keep the House of the Dragon sets and shooting secret.

(333) Catapults were powerful weapons used during medieval times to launch projectiles at enemy fortifications or troops. They were designed to hurl large rocks, fireballs, or other objects with great force and accuracy.

(334) Some fans joked that, in season two of House of the Dragon, Corlys spent so long loading that ship it is probably too heavy to float!

(335) Abigail Thorn, who plays Sharako Lohar, is the creator of the YouTube channel Philosophy Tube.

(336) Rhaenys interrupting Aegon's coronation was a scene invented for the television show. It isn't in the book.

(337) Although he is a great fan of historical fiction, this was not the approach that George RR Martin decided to take with his books. He wanted to create a fantasy world with the freedom to do as he wanted - while still inspired by some real historical events.

(338) In the hunting scene in season one we see dogs wearing leather armour. They actually used to do this in medieval times.

(339) Otto Hightower is more sinister and Machiavellian in the television show than he is in the book.

(340) Ryan Condal said he doesn't take the viewers for granted with House of the Dragon. He doesn't assume they have the Game of Thrones audience in the bag. He said he is well aware that the show has to be good or they'll go and watch something else.

(341) House of the Dragon arrived on HBO just as their acclaimed show Succession was coming to an end. Succession is about the corporate backstabbing which abounds when a family and their rivals battle and plot for control of a media company. House of the Dragon is sometimes described as a medieval Succession with swords and dragons!

(342) Fabian Wagner is the cinematographer on House of the Dragon.

(343) Oldtown is the seat of House Hightower.

(344) Vhagar is a green dragon.

(345) St Cuthbert's Cave in Cornwall has been used for location filming in House of the Dragon.

(346) Milly Alcock and Emily Carey did not know each before House of the Dragon. When they were cast as Rhaenyra and Alicent they arranged to meet up a couple of times before shooting so that they wouldn't be strangers on the set for the first day.

(347) Ser Criston Cole is an expert jouster.

(348) It was very difficult in House of the Dragon to fix all the

swords in place around the Iron Throne. They had to use metal rods and plaster.

(349) The design of Harrenhal in House of the Dragon was inspired by very old churches and cathedrals.

(350) On his blog, George RR Martin said that he thought The Red Dragon and the Gold had the best dragon battles ever put on film.

(351) The first two seasons of House of the Dragon cover about 40% of Dance of the Dragons.

(352) Matt Smith said Daemon is not the most evil character he has played because he was also once Patrick Bateman (from American Psycho) on the stage.

(353) HBO's streaming service is the third largest in America after Netflix and Amazon.

(354) House of the Dragon's second season only having eight episodes is often alleged to have been a consequence of the Warner Bros. Discovery merger. The new boss apparently wanted to tighten some belts when it came to costs.

(355) Storm's End is the seat of House Baratheon.

(356) The hunting trip in Second of His Name is not in the book and was an invention of the television show.

(357) Despite his vast acting experience, Bill Paterson (who plays Lyman Beesbury) was nervous on his first day of shooting House of the Dragon.

(358) House Hightower and House Velaryon did not appear in

Game of Thrones.

(359) Valyria is based on Ancient Rome.

(360) Unlike the characters in House of the Dragon, Daenerys Targaryen didn't have a saddle when she rode her dragons. She just had to cling on for dear life.

(361) Harrenhal was built by Harren the Black, a fearsome king in the Age of Heroes.

(362) You can buy House of the Dragon mouse pads.

(363) The Velaryons have a long-standing alliance with House Targaryen.

(364) You can buy House of the Dragon dragonfruit pomegranate cider.

(365) George RR Martin owns a home in Santa Fe, New Mexico, where he writes and has a large collection of memorabilia and artifacts from his career.

(366) The art of forging Valyrian steel was lost in a cataclysmic event known as the Doom of Valyria.

(367) Some of the cast on House of the Dragon have said they sometimes listen to music to get in the right frame of mind for a scene.

(368) Matt Smith said he felt much more pressure on Doctor Who than House of the Dragon because in Doctor Who he was the lead whereas with House of the Dragon he is part of a large ensemble.

(369) Steve Toussaint's first acting gig on the stage was in the pantomime Aladdin in 1990. One of his co-stars in the panto was the late John Inman - who famously played Mr Humphries in the vintage sitcom Are You Being Served?

(370) Emily Carey wore a Fendi couture dress to the London premiere of the first season.

(371) When the first season finished shooting, Olivia Cooke was asked in an interview what she wanted to do next and replied by saying that all she wanted to do was go on holiday and eat a lot of pasta!

(372) Emma D'Arcy won the IMDb STARmeter Award for 'Breakout Star' in 2022.

(373) Ewan Mitchell said that when transforms into Aemond he doesn't recognise himself in the mirror anymore. He said this is great for the process of losing yourself in a character.

(374) Emily Carey said she was only given scripts for her scenes when she played Alicent in House of the Dragon. She had no idea what else was happening in the show.

(375) Olivia Cooke wore a Stella McCartney dress to the London premiere of season two.

(376) You can buy Targaryen Pajama Pants online.

(377) Sam C. Wilson and Mark Stobbart, who play Blood & Cheese, had to keep their casting in House of the Dragon secret for an entire year.

(378) When he was asked on The Tonight Show who would win in a fight between Daemon and Jon Snow, Matt Smith

pointed out that Daemon has a dragon! I suppose you could counter that by saying that Jon Snow sort of had a dragon too in the end.

(379) Milly Alcock said she had no idea she was going to have such a leading role at the start of House of the Dragon. She just presumed she'd be in a few young Rhaenyra flashback scenes.

(380) After the release of House of the Dragon in 2022, Milly Alcock's Instagram followers jumped from a few thousand to 1.5 million in a matter of days.

(381) Emma D'Arcy and Olivia Cooke were both cast before Milly Alcock and Emily Carey were chosen to play the younger versions of their characters Rhaenyra and Allicent.

(382) Paddy Considine said that Viserys is the best character he has ever played.

(383) The Iron Throne in the books is made up of a 1000 swords.

(384) The dwarf Mushroom is one of the sources of the Targaryen history in Fire & Blood and served (as a fool) at the courts of Viserys I Targaryen, Aegon II Targaryen, Rhaenyra Targaryen, and Aegon III Targaryen. This character (save for what seems to be a very brief cameo in season one) does not feature in House of the Dragon. It could be the case that they didn't want this character in the show to avoid drawing comparisons to Peter Dinklage and Tyrion.

(385) The Faith of the Seven is the predominant religion in the Seven Kingdoms of Westeros. It is a polytheistic religion that worships seven gods, each representing a different aspect of

life. These gods are the Father, the Mother, the Warrior, the Maiden, the Smith, the Crone, and the Stranger.

(386) Game of Thrones and House of the Dragon clearly takes some influence from I, Claudius. I, Claudius is a historical novel written by Robert Graves, first published in 1934. It is a fictional autobiography of the Roman emperor Claudius, who ruled from 41 to 54 AD. The novel is written as if it were Claudius' own memoirs, recounting his life from childhood to his unexpected rise to power. The book provides a detailed insight into the political intrigue and scandals of ancient Rome. The book was turned into a brilliant television series by the BBC in 1976. The political intrigue and quest for power in Rome is a lot like the political intrigue and backstabbing we see in Kings Landing in Game of Thrones.

(387) The Wall symbolises the boundary between civilisation and the unknown.

(388) Greyscale is an infectious disease that causes the skin to turn into scales and stone  or something much like it.

(389) The Hall of Nine is the main hall of High Tide.

(390) Olivia Cooke said the Red Keep set can get a bit chilly.

(391) Ryan Condal said he would love House of the Dragon to come out each summer but said it is impossible to produce the show that quickly.

(392) House of the Dragon's production employs some medieval military advisors.

(393) Milly Alcock said she grew to love horses through working on House of the Dragon.

(394) Matt Smith said he is quite fond of Daemon Targaryen - despite the bad things he has done.

(395) At the New York premiere of season two, guests were served a dragon-inspired take on a spicy margarita.

(396) There is a general perception that season two of House of the Dragon span its wheels a bit too much and didn't progress the story as much as some might have hoped.

(397) The friendship between Jacaerys and Cregan from the book seems to have been largely jettisoned in the television show.

(398) Sam C. Wilson, who played Blood in House of the Dragon, was probably best known for his role as Bill Sikes in the television show Dodger.

(399) Vhagar is the most battle hardened and dangerous dragon.

(400) Olivia Cooke described House of the Dragon as a bit like a kitchen sink drama on an epic scale!

(401) Matthew Needham wore a Brioni suit to the London premiere of season two.

(402) Olivia Cooke said she doesn't really have anything in common with Alicent in real life. Olivia said Alicent is a traditionalist who likes things to stay the same - an attitude which Olivia does not share.

(403) Matt Smith said that Daemon Targaryen is a man who lives his life on the 'edge' of a knife.

(404) Fire & Blood is written as a historical account by Archmaester Gyldayn.

(405) The Targaryens are depicted as both formidable and flawed in their quest for dominion. Their ambition leads to both glorious victories and catastrophic failures.

(406) The dragon is often seen as a representation of total power and control in various military insignias and emblems.

(407) You can buy a House of the Dragon Fleece Sofa Blanket.

(408) In the episode King of the Narrow Sea, Matt Smith and Milly Alcock only saw all the naked extras at the brothel when they shot the scene. They did this so that their reactions would be more genuine.

(409) We never saw Storm's End in Game of Thrones but we do see it in House of the Dragon.

(410) Harren the Black thought that Harrenhal would protect him from the Targaryens but he didn't account for dragon fire.

(411) The crew on House of the Dragon took two weeks to get their equipment on the tidal island of St Micheal's Mount in Cornwall.

(412) Ryan Condal was a writer on the Dwayne Johnson films Hercules and Rampage.

(413) Paddy Considine worked as a photographer before he became an actor.

(414) In the book, unlike the television show, there is no scene

where Daemon kills his wife.

(415) Ryan Condal said he avoids looking at social media posts about House of the Dragon.

(416) 1:26 Pictures is the name of the production company who make House of the Dragon with HBO.

(417) If you count the dream sequence, Paddy Considine was in ten episodes of House of the Dragon.

(418) The Pink Dread is the name of the pig given to Aemond as a prank.

(419) Jefferson Hall, who plays the Lannister twins in House of the Dragon, said he didn't base his performance on the Lannister characters in Game of Thrones. He simply tried to do his own thing.

(420) Monsanto in Portugal was an especially appropriate location for House of the Dragon because it has a wonderful medieval clock tower.

(421) There are already location tours for some of the places where House of the Dragon has filmed.

(422) Matt Smith jokingly described the characters in House of the Dragon as a bunch of maniacs in wigs!

(423) George RR Martin was very enthusiastic about the Red Keep set built for House of the Dragon. On his blog he said it was more impressive than some real castles he had visited.

(424) A painted backdrop was used for the Battle of the Stepstones to depict high cliffs in the background.

(425) Ryan Condal said the Small Council scenes are among the most difficult to write on House of the Dragon.

(426) An article on Literary Hub ranked Smaug from The Hobbit and Kalessin from The Farthest Shore as the greatest fictional dragons.

(427) The Targaryens have used sibling marriages to keep their bloodline pure.

(428) Bill Paterson, who plays Lyman Beesbury, was once in an episode of Doctor Who with Matt Smith.

(429) You can buy 'Officially Licensed House of the Dragon Targaryen Dragonborn' coffee. The blurb goes like this - 'A premium coffee blend that will transport you to the fiery world of Westeros. Made from the finest Arabica beans, it has a bold, rich flavor with notes of spiced rum, butterscotch, and caramel. It will surely awaken your senses.'

(430) It took 40 years to build the castle at Harrenhal.

(431) In the book, Daemon spends three years fighting the Crabfeeder. The television show has Daemon banishing the Crabfeeder more swiftly.

(432) The dragons in House of The Dragon are very independent creatures. They can't be tamed but they will develop a bond with a specific human.

(433) Olivia Cooke said she finds it quite amusing that thanks to House of the Dragon she played her first grandmother role in her late twenties!

(434) Guns and gunpowder do not seem to exist in House of

the Dragon and Game of Thrones.

(435) The marketing campaign for season two of House of the Dragon was themed around the phrase 'Raise Your Banners'.

(436) The Heirs of the Dragon is a chapter title in Fire & Blood.

(437) Dragonstone is notable for its distinctive black stone and the presence of dragon motifs throughout its architecture.

(438) After it was captured by Aegon the Conqueror, Harrenhal fell into disrepair. It has a reputation as an unlucky place.

(439) You can buy a House of the Dragon Crown Laptop Sleeve.

(440) George RR Martin's work often eschews typical fantasy tropes like guaranteed happy endings or the triumph of good over evil. Instead, it presents a harsher reality where not every character makes it to the end, and victories may come at a high cost.

(441) You can buy Kross Studio House of the Dragon watches. Each watch is inspired by a different dragon.

(442) Olivia Cooke wore a sequined gown by Thom Browne to the Los Angeles premiere of season two.

(443) The Red Keep is known for its iconic towers.

(444) Some believe dragons are based on the discovery of large dinosaur fossils that ancient people misinterpreted as giant reptiles.

(445) Olivia Cooke thinks she has got a lot better as an actor since her early days.

(446) Eve Best is a highly acclaimed stage actor.

(447) The Targaryens' control over dragons is symbolic of their dominion over the Seven Kingdoms.

(448) Vhagar is known as the Queen of All Dragons.

(449) A Knight of the Seven Kingdoms, the second spin-off show from Game of Thrones, was based at Titanic Studios in Belfast where Game of Thrones was made. They obviously couldn't use Leavesden studios because House of the Dragon was already based there.

(450) Castles are designed to withstand siege warfare, with thick walls, towers, and other defensive structures to withstand attacks from enemies.

(451) House of the Dragon didn't quite manage to win the summer streaming battle of 2024 because The Boys took the number one slot.

(452) The cast on House of the Dragon are assigned continuity people who explain where exactly the overall story is before a specific scene.

(453) House of the Dragon has won BAFTAS for sound, make-up, and special effects.

(454) Matt Smith said he wasn't really aware of the hype or anticipation for House of the Dragon because they were all in a little bubble in Leavesden just getting on with their jobs.

(455) House of the Dragon has won a Golden Globe for best television drama.

(456) Steve Toussaint changed his surname because it clashed with another actor. He chose Toussaint because of the Haitian revolutionary leader Toussaint Louverture.

(457) House of the Dragon has been nominated for four Saturn Awards.

(458) Not a single episode in season one of House of the Dragon scored under eight on IMDB. However, the truncated season two has four episodes which scored less than eight.

(459) Ewan Mitchell never went to drama school.

(460) Emily Carey's first acting job was in a West End production of Shrek when she was eight years old.

(461) Olivia Cooke wore Givenchy's floor-length dress to the Paris premiere of season two.

(462) Rhys Ifans wore a Fendi Spring 2024 suit to the London premiere of season two.

(463) Fabien Frankel said he had to get into good shape for the sword fighting antics in House of the Dragon.

(464) HBO lost a lot of viewers when Game of Thrones came to an end after eight seasons. The elusive search for the 'next Game of Thrones' unavoidably saw them return to the books of George RR Martin.

(465) The character Blood is a disgraced Gold Cloak.

(466) HBO have an awful lot riding on House of the Dragon because if it is ever deemed a middling show or loses viewers then that might put future spin-offs in peril.

(467) Fabien Frankel said when he was cast in House of the Dragon the first thing he did was telephone his mother to tell her the good news.

(468) Matt Smith said he thinks that Daemon enjoys being the 'black sheep' of his family.

(469) George RR Martin gave the cast members on House of the Dragon a signed copy of Fire & Blood.

(470) Milly Alcock was born in the year 2000. Her star sign is Aries.

(471) A season can last for years in Westeros.

(472) Rhaenyra Targaryen became known as the Half-Year Queen in the book.

(473) Despite leaving the show, Paddy Considine keeps up to date with House of the Dragon and often posts about it on social media.

(474) Olivia Cooke said the cast on House of the Dragon are very close and all get on.

(475) Extras on House of the Dragon say you have a better chance of being hired if you have a beard.

(476) There are a lot more swords in and around the Iron Throne in House of the Dragon than there were in Game of Thrones.

(477) Dracarys is High Valyrian for 'dragonfire'.

(478) The Iron Throne in the books is bigger than the one in the show.

(479) House of the Dragon production designer Jim Clay said a lot of effort went into making the castles in the show feel different from one another with their distinct personality and atmosphere.

(480) You could probably describe House of the Dragon as HBO's current flagship show.

(481) House of the Dragon skips over a lot of history in Fire & Blood in order to focus on the Dance of the Dragons.

(482) Memory, Sorrow, and Thorn by Tad Williams was an influence on George RR Martin writing the books. Memory, Sorrow, and Thorn is a high fantasy series consisting of three books: The Dragonbone Chair, Stone of Farewell, and To Green Angel Tower. The series follows the story of a young man named Simon who embarks on an epic quest to save his kingdom from a powerful evil force known as the Storm King.

(483) It took two months to create the Iron Throne seen in the show.

(484) During the Changing of the Guard at Buckingham Palace in 2014, the Queen's guards performed the Game of Thrones theme.

(485) The land north of the wall is a vast area bigger than the United States.

(486) A lot of the weapons in the show were actually made of

rubber so that no one would get hurt.

(487) George RR Martin said it is very deliberate the characters in House of the Dragon are 'grey' and murky when it comes to a moral compass.

(488) The Iron Throne is made up of swords taken from the enemies of the king who sits on it.

(489) Matt Smith is the youngest actor to play the Doctor in Doctor Who. He was only 26 when he auditioned for the part.

(490) The Vale is a mountainous region known for its beautiful landscapes and rich resources.

(491) You can buy House Targaryen Stainless Steel Cufflinks online.

(492) The iconic Iron Throne in the show was made of fiberglass covered in a metallic paint to give it a realistic look.

(493) Ewan Mitchell plays Olivia Cooke's son in House of the Dragon but in real life Ewan is only a year younger than Olivia.

(494) HBO refused the temptation (if there was any) of putting House of the Dragon strictly on HBO Max.

(495) Holywell Beach in Cornwall was used in House of the Dragon.

(496) Ryan Condal, the showrunner on House of the Dragon, said that his favourite Game of Thrones character was the Hound.

(497) George RR Martin said the immense fame the television shows gave him has been a mixed blessing.

(498) House of the Dragon first season star Milly Alcock was later cast as Supergirl in the DC film universe.

(499) Matt Smith said he injured his neck shooting the first season because of the fights and stunts.

(500) King's Landing is the capital city of the Seven Kingdoms. It is located on the eastern coast of Westeros and serves as the seat of the Iron Throne, the ruling monarchy of the realm. King's Landing is a bustling and highly populated city, known for its political intrigue, power struggles, and lavish lifestyles of the noble families who reside there. Life for ordinary folk is a bit less lavish though to say the least.

(501) You can buy prop House of the Dragon swords and shields online.

(502) Emma D'Arcy describes themselves as very introverted and said interviews and press tours for the show are not easy.

(503) The Iron Throne was redesigned for House of the Dragon and looks somewhat different to how it looked in Game of Thrones.

(504) George RR Martin is a big fan of the film Dragonslayer. It may well have influenced him having dragons in his books.

(505) Some of the costumes for House of the Dragon took months to make.

(506) It is estimated that George RR Martin earns about $15 million a year in revenue.

(507) There is something supernatural about dragons in George RR Martin's work in the way they bond with a human rider and hatch in unfathomable ways suggestive of sacrifice and blood magic.

(508) House of the Dragon's Instagram has (at the time of writing) 2 million followers.

(509) Emma D'Arcy had no idea at first that they were auditioning for a Game of Thrones spin-off. Emma actually thought it was an unrelated Game of Thrones 'rip-off' at first!

(510) The dragon antics in House of the Dragon were increased somewhat in season two.

(511) Emma D'Arcy said they don't really get recognised in public due to having short hair - which is obviously very different from Rhaenyra.

(512) Matt Smith said he was hesitant to do House of the Dragon at first because he wasn't sure trying to follow Game of Thrones was a great idea.

(513) Dinorwic and Trefor quarries in Snowdonia were deployed for the exteriors of Dragonstone and Harrenhal castles.

(514) Ty Tennant is the stepson of former Doctor Who actor David Tennant.

(515) Season two of House of the Dragon took five and a half months to shoot. This was shorter than the production of season one because this time there were no covid complications.

(516) Prince-Admiral Craghas Drahar is known as the Crabfeeder due to his habit of feeding his enemies to the crabs.

(517) Vhagar is both the largest and oldest dragon in Westeros.

(518) It is probably fair to say that Game of Thrones had way more humour than House of the Dragon. There were funny characters and lines in Game of Thrones but not so much in House of the Dragon.

(519) The 'dragons' on the set were just a pole with a ball attached - which the actors had to look at, react to, and pretend was a dragon. The dragons were obviously added in later with digital special effects.

(520) HBO (Home Box Office) is a premium cable and streaming service known for its original programming.

(521) Holywell Bay near Newquay in Cornwall was also used in the television show Poldark and the Bond film Die Another Day.

(522) There are big time jumps in the first season of House of the Dragon - which some viewers found a trifle confusing.

(523) Game of Thrones stars Natalie Dormer and John Bradley and House of the Dragon star Matt Smith were all in a terrible horror film called Patient Zero.

(524) Emily Carey said that she and Paddy Considine bonded by watching Drag Race together.

(525) Olivia Cooke said she was sold on House of the Dragon

after reading the first two scripts.

(526) Paddy Considine has a rock band called Riding The Low.

(527) The casting director on House of the Dragon was Kate Rhodes James. She said she cast Emma D' Arcy because she wanted someone 'unusual' for Rhaenyra and not your typical 'doe eyed' television leading lady.

(528) Eve Best, who played Princess Rhaenys Velaryon in House of the Dragon, had never watched Game of Thrones when she was cast in the prequel.

(529) Emily Carey said she is not into the fantasy genre much herself as a viewer and much prefers romantic comedies.

(530) Ryan Condal likened the Targaryens to the Jedi in Star Wars in that they were powerful and their dynasty is like a sort of half remembered myth.

(531) HBO's decision to move ahead with Game of Thrones spin-offs was obviously motivated in large part by wanting a big IP for their streaming service.

(532) There were eight different visual effects houses working on the FX for season two of House of the Dragon.

(533) Ryan Condal defended the relative lack of action in season two by saying he didn't have unlimited resources and was still putting the story in place before the really crazy stuff happens.

(534) Paddy Considine declined an audition for Game of Thrones because he wasn't interested in doing a fantasy show and didn't really know what he was being offered. He would of

course years later play Viserys I Targaryen in the prequel show.

(535) George RR Martin said it is very intentional in House of the Dragon that working out who is the hero and who is the villain is confusing at times to say the least.

(536) The Iron Throne symbolises power, authority, and the constant struggle for dominance.

(537) You can actually buy a Game of Thrones cheese board online!

(538) In the books the White Walkers are known as the 'Others'.

(539) The sigil of House Tully is a silver trout emerging over waves.

(540) Some fans of Fire & Blood are doubtful that House of the Dragon can do justice to everything that happens in just four seasons.

(541) Milly Alcock said House of the Dragon was actually the quickest audition process she has ever been through.

(542) Matt Smith was in 44 episodes of Doctor Who. He said he left because he felt it was time to try something else as an actor.

(543) Some blamed HBO penny pinching for the lack of action in season two but this is a trifle unfair because in relative terms House of the Dragon is a very expensive show.

(544) The scene with Blood and Cheese is sort of like the 'Red

Wedding' of Fire & Blood and its arrival in House of the Dragon was highly anticipated.

(545) Ewan Mitchell wore an Alexander McQueen rust velvet coat to the London premiere of season two.

(546) They actually put up a fake temporary castle prop for the Leicester Square premiere of season one.

(547) One of the premieres for season one took place at Beurs van Berlage in Amsterdam. This is a 19th-century former grain exchange.

(548) Steve Toussaint, who plays Lord Corlys Velaryon, said House of the Dragon is different from Game of Thrones because the focus of the prequel is about the self-inflicted destruction of a family.

(549) Paddy Considine said he was attracted to House of the Dragon because it didn't feel like a 'mere spin-off' and seemed strong enough to stand on its own feet and justify its existence.

(550) The premiere episode of House of the Dragon in 2022 got double the amount of viewers than the premiere episode of Stranger Things 4.

(551) In the book, Maelor is the surviving child from the Blood & Cheese scene. In the television show though Maelor has yet to be born.

(552) You can buy a lovely art packed book called The Rise of the Dragon: An Illustrated History of the Targaryen Dynasty.

(553) House of the Dragon and other shows of a similar ilk had

some of their thunder stolen in 2024 by the FX show Shōgun. Shōgun (based on the 1975 novel by James Clavell) was described by many as sort of like Game of Thrones (minus the fantasy elements) only set in Japan in the year 1600.

(554) There have been some House of the Dragon themed pop up bars.

(555) HBO Max now seems to be known simply as Max.

(556) The Blood & Cheese scene is a lot more graphic and distressing in the book than it is in the television show.

(557) Fabien Frankel is sometimes photographed by castmates having a nap on the set of House of the Dragon. Wearing that armour obviously makes him sleepy!

(558) The French newspaper Le Monde described season two of House of the Dragon as a 'grand spectacle of frustration'.

(559) Vermithor was previously ridden by King Jaehaerys.

(560) You can buy a House of the Dragon Horn Mug online.

(561) Moondancer and Vermax are the youngest dragons.

(562) Kynance Cove was used for where House Velaryon is located. Kynance Cove is a cove on the eastern side of Mount's Bay, Cornwall, England.

(563) It has been alleged that the original plan for season two (before HBO cut the season to eight episodes) was to end with the Battle of the Gullet and the fall of King's Landing.

(564) Mark Stobbart, who plays Cheese, got his first screen

credit playing Jimmy Nail's son in the popular British show Auf Wiedersehen, Pet.

(565) The older Rhaenyra is quite plump in the book after having children.

(566) A few years before he landed Doctor Who, Matt Smith unsuccessfully auditioned for the lead part in the fantasy show Merlin.

(567) The second season finale has a mediocre score of 50% on Rotten Tomatoes.

(568) Some fans (though not all obviously) think House of the Dragon should have been a three season show which cut to the chase a lot quicker.

(569) The Red Keep is a mighty symbol of power.

(570) At the New York premiere of season two, a giant Weirwood tree was the centrepiece of the party.

(571) George RR Martin said he hopes there is a sort of 'Marvel universe' of television shows based on his books.

(572) Matt Smith is a supporter of the football team Blackburn Rovers.

(573) There are six rather than seven kingdoms at the time House of the Dragon takes place.

(574) Streams of Game of Thrones online saw a big spike as the premiere of House of the Dragon neared in 2022. It seems a lot of people were doing a Thrones re-watch as they waited for the prequel.

(575) You can buy a Blackfyre 'hero prop' sword online.

(576) The bucking bronco device the actors use for dragon riding scenes lifts them six feet off the ground so it can be quite an alarming experience until you get used to it.

(577) Milly Alcock has a brief appearance as the young Rhaenyra in season two of House of the Dragon. Milly was able to spare two days to shoot this cameo.

(578) Some feel that House of the Dragon feels smaller and more constrictive than Game of Thrones because it has less locations and fewer characters.

(579) In the books it is said that Rhaenyra Targaryen was a great beauty as a teenager but became dumpy and tired looking after having children.

(580) Ryan Condal said season two of House of the Dragon was a metaphor for nuclear conflict. There is a tense Cold War with everyone on the brink.

(581) Valyrian Steel is one of the few substances that can kill White Walkers.

(582) The sigil of House Stark is a grey direwolf on a white field.

(583) House Tully is a noble family in the Riverlands of Westeros.

(584) You can buy a dog toy seat based on the Iron Throne.

(585) Game of Thrones star Lena Headey said she doesn't watch House of the Dragon because it would be too 'weird'.

(586) Emma D'Arcy studied Fine Art at the University of Oxford's art school.

(587) George RR Martin said that Winterfell is his favourite castle.

(588) You can see a dragon theme in some of the chairs and decor at King's Landing in Game of Thrones. This indicates that the Lannisters kept some of the Targaryen furnishings in place.

(589) Ryan Condal said he finds Ser Criston Cole a very interesting character because Criston is a self-made man and had no privilege or family connections to fall back on.

(590) You can buy House of the Dragon keyrings on Etsy.

(591) House of the Dragon's second season only having eight episodes seems to be increasingly common in television. Shows are becoming increasingly expensive to produce so it is not economically viable to make long seasons as happened in the past.

(592) George RR Martin took a degree of inspiration from the Lord of the Rings books.

(593) House of the Dragon has a much more consistent look in terms of lighting and photography than Game of Thrones because the focus is on a more constrictive location.

(594) At the time of writing, House of the Dragon has a very solid and above average rating of 8.4 on IMDB. This is below Game of Thrones though - which stands at 9.2

(595) Season two of House of the Dragon had a crew of 1,250

people.

(596) You can buy a House of The Dragon backpack online.

(597) HBO were said to be initially uneasy about the time jump and recasting of Rhaenyra and Alicent in season one but they thought it worked out well in the end.

(598) You can buy House of the Dragon themed rugs online.

(599) When the show first came out, there were red carpet House of the Dragon premiere screenings to generate buzz for the series in Europe.

(600) Olivia Cooke said she was initially daunted by the thought of being in House of the Dragon because she is wary of too much fame.

(601) Dragonstone is historically the seat of the heir apparent to the Iron Throne.

(602) Paddy Considine said that House of the Dragon helped him escape from forever being known as the 'man in the green coat' from Dead Man's Shoes. Dead Man's Shoes is a cult British film by Shane Meadows.

(603) House of the Dragon casting director Kate Rhodes James said her task was complicated by the fact it was very difficult to find any working British actors who hadn't been in Game of Thrones!

(604) You can buy a House of the Dragon wine glass online.

(605) Around the time that House of the Dragon takes place, the Lannisters are rich but not yet major players in Westeros.

(606) Each episode of House of the Dragon costs $20 million. This might explain why HBO chopped season two by two episodes. It saved them $40 million.

(607) Some dragon banners were put up in Grand Central Station to promote the show when season two came out.

(608) Early on in House of the Dragon, the Red Keep has risque frescoes on the wall as a symbol of the decadence of Targaryen rule.

(609) Emily Carey said that she wasn't allowed to tell anyone what she was acting in on the first few months of House of the Dragon. The cast sign NDA's - non-disclosure agreements.

(610) Caroline McCall took over as the lead costume designer in season two of House of the Dragon. Among the previous shows she had worked on was Downton Abbey.

(611) Some cultures believe that dreaming of dragons is a sign of good luck.

(612) The keep, or central stronghold of a castle, serves as the residence and last line of defense for the ruling leader and his family.

(613) You can buy a House Targaryen drinking goblet online.

(614) There was a deleted scene where Criston Cole inducted into the Kingsguard.

(615) Carly Wray, who had written for Westworld and Watchmen, was initially going to be the showrunner on what became House of the Dragon. Wray apparently left the project though due to differences with George RR Martin over which

Targaryen timeline the show should adopt at the beginning. (616) HBO signed a deal with George RR Martin in 2021 which apparently stipulates spin-off shows from Game of Thrones must be approved by him. Their desire to bring Martin more 'into the loop' as an advisor was thought to stem from the poor reception to the ending of Game of Thrones.

(617) Game of Thrones showrunners David Benioff and D. B. Weiss, doubtless bruised from the reception to the last season of Game of Thrones and weary of spending so long working on this type of show, wanted nothing to do with any prequels. After their planned Star Wars film failed to transpire they laid low for a while and then made the 3 Body Problem science fiction adaptation for Netflix.

(618) There is a scene in Game of Thrones where Shireen Baratheon is reading a book about the Dance of the Dragons.

(619) The audience score for House of the Dragon on Rotten Tomatoes is a pretty decent 79%.

(620) Though it generally got pretty good reviews, some critics complained that the pacing of scenes in season one of House of the Dragon was too glacial.

(621) Yr Eifl Granite Quarry in Gwynedd was one of the locations used to depict Dragonstone.

(622) Some critics complained that, unlike Game of Thrones, House of the Dragon doesn't really give you any likeable characters to root for.

(623) George RR Martin said he approved of the way they handled the 'time jumps' in season one of House of the Dragon.

(624) Meleys is regarded to be the fastest dragon.

(625) The Battle of the Gullet is a mighty sea battle fought between ships and dragons.

(626) George RR Martin said he doesn't like the current fad for taking old books and editing them to remove content deemed dated or offensive.

(627) You can buy House Stark Direwolf Sigil Bookholders online.

(628) Swords made of Valyrian Steel are highly sought after and often passed down through noble families for generations.

(629) More people watched the season two finale of House of the Dragon than watched the season two premiere.

(630) The north is the largest region of Westeros.

(631) Milly Alcock got her start doing commercials. She did one for KFC among others.

(632) Though the show was still in the early stages of production at the time, HBO released a small House of the Dragon teaser to mark an anniversary of Game of Thrones.

(633) Driftmark is the biggest island in Blackwater Bay.

(634) Tom Glynn-Carney and Ty Tennant played the same character at different ages previously in the film Tolkien.

(635) House of the Dragon was the most streamed show in the month of July 2024.

(636) House of the Dragon is not though the overall most streamed show of its era. Bridgerton has nearly double the amount of streaming views of House of the Dragon.

(637) The scene in season two where Rhaenyra sneaks into King's Landing got some criticism from fans for not making much sense. Ryan Condal seemed to imply that the motivation for this scene was him wanting Emma D'Arcy and Olivia Cooke to have some screen time together.

(638) Matt Smith said that making a popular television show today is more difficult than it was in the glory years of Game of Thrones because the market is so 'saturated' and there are now more new television shows than any one person could ever find the time to watch.

(639) In 2018, characters from Game of Thrones appeared on postage stamps in Britain.

(640) Nikolaj Coster-Waldau, who played Jamie Lannister in Game of Thrones, said it was very surreal for him to watch the first House of the Dragon trailer.

(641) Gavin Spokes, who plays Lyonel Strong, said House of the Dragon had more 'meat on the bones' than Game of Thrones and was a deeper show.

(642) George RR Martin said having his characters adapted into television shows by other writers is a bit like having your kids adopted!

(643) Hartland in North Devon has been used for location shooting in House of the Dragon.

(644) Olivia Cooke said she had a slight hangover on her first

day shooting House of the Dragon because she'd drunk a bottle of wine the night before.

(645) Fabien Frankel said he was so overwhelmed when he was told he had got a part in House of the Dragon that he thought he was going to faint.

(646) If you've read the book you already know what happens to the characters in House of the Dragon but there is the possibility that the television show might subvert a few expectations.

(647) At the New York premiere of season two, chocolate covered popcorn was given to guests as they watched the episode.

(648) Matt Smith said he tends to steer clear of reading reviews on anything he was in.

(649) In 2023 it was calculated that there still are about 70 million google searches a year for Game of Thrones.

(650) Ewan Mitchell said he avoided eye contact with Matt Smith on the set initially because he wanted to see him only as Daemon.

(651) Matt Smith's teenage dream of becoming a footballer was scuppered by a back injury.

(652) A few entertainment sites alleged that the reason why Miguel Sapochnik left his role as co-showrunner/director on House of the Dragon is that his request for his wife to join the producing team was denied.

(653) Matt Smith said he did talk to Emilia Clarke before doing

House of the Dragon. They were actually in that terrible Terminator film together - though Matt's scenes were largely cut from the picture.

(654) Olivia Cooke and Freddie Fox both appeared in the series Slow Horses.

(655) The Valyrian steel dagger of Viserys is the one used by Arya in Game of Thrones.

(656) Luke and Elliott Tittensor, who played Sir Arryk and Sir Erryk, said they tried to steal as many props as they could while on the show!

(657) You can buy a limited edition replica of the crown of King Viserys I Targaryen.

(658) Eve Best said that, on the House of the Dragon set, Paddy Considine disliked anyone else sitting on the Iron Throne!

(659) Game of Thrones only featured three dragons. Dragons were thought to be extinct when Game of Thrones begins.

(660) Olivia Cooke said she has to wear so many garments as Alicent that using the toilet is a nightmare!

(661) George RR Martin said the characters in House of the Dragon are motivated by power and jealousy.

(662) Milly Alcock has blonde hair in real life - though obviously not as white blonde as a Targaryen.

(663) The Vale is surrounded by mountains - thus affording it natural defences.

(664) The second season of House of the Dragon averaged 25 million cross-platform viewers.

(665) Though some fans (who might understandably be a bit weary of endless prequels in popular culture) would like to see a spin-off set after season eight of Game of Thrones the obvious problem with that is that the actors from Game of Thrones have moved onto other things. It would be a question of who was willing to come back and who was available.

Such complications are a salient reason why it is much easier to just do a prequel with a new cast.

(666) One of the things about George RR Martin's books which make them so gripping is the sense of danger. It made us feel that few of the characters were safe.

(667) The Iron Throne in the show is very uncomfortable to sit on.

(668) There is more diffused light in House of the Dragon than Game of Thrones. Diffused light, or soft light, is light that's filtered by something.

(669) Because the Red Keep set for House of the Dragon was built to be connected like a real castle interior, the directors on the show can shoot in any direction they want.

(670) The two 'dual' trailers for season two of House of the Dragon had 80 million views in the first 72 hours.

(671) As far as kings in George RR Martin's stories go, Viserys I Targaryen is kind and decent.

(672) Jamie Kenna, who plays Ser Alfred Broome, was initially

told his audition was unsuccessful but about three weeks later they changed their mind and cast him.

(673) Warner Bros. Studios at Leavesden added new stages and a wraparound LED room in 2021. House of the Dragon was the first production to take advantage of these new additions.

(674) Games of Thrones was occasionally cited as a show that wasn't diverse enough in its casting. House of the Dragon, by contrast, has more black cast members.

(675) House of the Dragon has three different shooting units who can work separate from one another. A unit is made up of about 300 crew.

(676) An ice cream store in Australia celebrated the launch of House of the Dragon in 2022 with limited edition specials. The specials were 'Heir to the Cone' (red velvet cheesecake gelato with dragon fruit puree) and 'House Vanillaryon' (burnt vanilla gelato, smoked chocolate brownie and burnt honey caramel).

(677) There is a mud wrestling scene in season two. In the books though this takes place many years after the Dance of the Dragons.

(678) The cast on House of the Dragon have to log into a password protected database to read the scripts. Scripts are electronic to prevent one being stolen or leaked.

(679) Olivia Cooke said that you get 'timed out' after an hour when you access the House of the Dragon scripts - which can be frustrating because you then have to log back in.

(680) Olivia Cooke said on House of the Dragon they are given

printed 'sides' to read but they can't keep them. They have to be handed back. Sides are a portion of the script, typically just a couple of pages culled from one or more scenes.

(681) The Iron Throne in the books is much more elevated (to enable the king to look down on everyone).

(682) House of the Dragon production designer Jim Clay said all the interiors in the show came from sketches and drawings he had done.

(683) Valyrian Steel is said to be forged with spells and dragonfire in the ancient city of Valyria, and it is extremely rare in the world of Westeros.

(684) Were it not for HBO cutting the episode count from ten to eight, the second season of House of the Dragon would have had a more exciting ending. What basically happened was that a lot of stuff had to be pushed off in to the long grass until season three.

(685) George RR Martin said it was deliberate in House of the Dragon to give you no obvious character to root for.

(686) The sigil of House Baratheon is a stag.

(687) Matt Smith didn't watch Doctor Who growing up because it had been axed and wasn't on telly at the time.

(688) Olivia Cooke said it is a bit weird that the actors who play her children are around the same age as her in real life.

(689) Some critics feel that House of the Dragon takes itself a bit too seriously. There isn't much levity compared to Game of Thrones.

(690) Ryan Condal said on House of The Dragon they made a lot of effort to give each dragon their own character and personality.

(691) The food the men of the Night's Watch have to eat is notoriously bad.

(692) The book House of the Dragon is based on only gets to King Visery about half-way through.

(693) There was a rumour that Elizabeth Olsen (Wanda Maximoff in the Marvel film universe) was going to be in House of the Dragon but this was false. Elizabeth Olsen did have a connection to the franchise though because she unsuccessfully auditioned for the part of Daenerys in Game of Thrones.

(694) You can buy a House Targaryen Signet Ring online.

(695) Valyrian Steel is known for being incredibly sharp, strong, and valuable.

(696) It is hard to say why House of the Dragon cost so much less than Rings of Power. The general theory is that HBO have so much experience of making big fantasy shows they now do them very efficiently.

(697) Matt Smith said it would be impossible for House of the Dragon to replicate the mania and success of Game of Thrones. He said that they just wanted House of the Dragon to be thought of as a good show that had its own identity and was different to Game of Thrones.

(698) George RR Martin said that Westeros is about the size of South America.

(699) You can buy a range of House of the Dragon posters online for very reasonable prices.

(700) The Wall along the northern border of Westeros was inspired by Hadrian's Wall. Hadrian's Wall is a famous historical site located in northern England, built by the Roman Emperor Hadrian in the 2nd century AD. The wall was the northernmost boundary of the Roman Empire at the time. It was constructed to defend the Roman province of Britannia against raids from the 'barbarian' tribes to the north.

(701) Game of Thrones became a merchandising juggernaut. This was somewhat unusual for something which was aimed at mature audiences. House of the Dragon, though a mature show, has also done pretty well on the merch front.

(702) Matt Smith said playing the Doctor in Doctor Who was the hardest role he's ever played because there were so many lines to learn.

(703) Robert E. Howard was a big influence on George RR Martin. Robert E. Howard (1906-1936) was an American author best known for creating the character Conan the Barbarian. Howard is considered one of the pioneers of the sword and sorcery genre of fiction, and his work has had a major influence on the fantasy genre as a whole.

(704) According to data by Spin Genie, Game of Thrones is the most popular television show in history when you factor in viewers, social media interest, media articles etc. Stranger Things ranked second. It seems unlikely that House of the Dragon will manage to claw its way to this remarkable level of popularity.

(705) Emma D'Arcy is 5'7 tall.

(706) Matt Smith said that grief was the main theme of season two.

(707) George RR Martin said that Fritz Leiber was an influence on his work. Fritz Leiber (1910-1992) was an American writer known for his work in science fiction, fantasy, and horror. He is best known for his Fafhrd and the Gray Mouser series, which follows the adventures of two sword-and-sorcery heroes in the fictional world of Nehwon.

(708) Matt Smith said he missed the rest of the cast in season two when Daemon was stuck in Harrenhal.

(709) The kiss between Rhaenyra and Mysaria wasn't scripted or planned. Emma D'Arcy said it was an 'organic' moment.

(710) George RR Martin was a television writer in his younger years. Among the shows he worked on was Beauty and the Beast - a late 1980s fantasy show with Linda Hamilton and Ron Perlman.

(711) Matt Smith auditioned to play Dr Watson in Steven Moffat's show Sherlock. Smith was deemed too eccentric to be a good foil for Benedict Cumberbatch but Moffat clearly took note of Smith because he cast him as the lead in Doctor Who. Matt Smith definitely seemed more like a Sherlock Holmes than a Dr Watson.

(712) Mead is an alcoholic beverage made by fermenting honey with water. It is often referred to as honey wine.

(713) Sara Hess, a writer and producer on House of the Dragon, said that Abigail Thorn as Sharako Lohar was designed to being some 'fun' and 'levity' into what can be a 'grim' show.

(714) George RR Martin said that House of the Dragon would need forty episodes to tell its story.

(715) The Guardian newspaper described House of the Dragon's season two finale as 'aggressively' anti-climactic.

(716) Giving birth in House of the Dragon is a dangerous business. This is taken from medieval times - where you had a 50/50 chance of surviving childbirth.

(717) George RR Martin said he is unlikely to write any scripts for House of the Dragon as he was too busy working on his own (much delayed) book.

(718) Olivia Cooke said she is a bit envious of the other characters riding dragons because she wouldn't mind a go on the mechanical bull.

(719) Ryan Condal said the Battle of the Gullet didn't feature in season two because they wanted to wait and give the battle the 'time and space' required to do it justice.

(720) Prestige and popular HBO shows had much longer seasons in the past. The Sopranos, for example, ran to thirteen episodes a season.

(721) Some (though obviously not all) fans have complained that House of the Dragon, compared to the book, is bending over backwards to make the women seem peaceable and reasonable and the men war mongering idiots.

(722) Dragons can fly faster than ravens.

(723) George RR Martin said he had the power to snub Hollywood and choose HBO to adapt his books because he

didn't need the money. The question of who would pay him the most didn't come into the equation

(724) Olivia Cooke said, in preparation for House of the Dragon, she binged the whole of Game of Thrones with her mother.

(725) You can buy House of the Dragon pint glasses.

(726) House of the Dragon is different from Game of Thrones in that the endgame and time it will run was known by the showrunner in advance.

(727) The mechanical seat the actors have to sit on for dragon riding scenes is known as the 'buck' on the set.

(728) Ryan Condal said it was unavoidably daunting having to do the first show which span off from Game of Thrones because he knew the expectations were going to be high.

(729) The Wall is 1,000 leagues from King's Landing. It takes an hour to walk a single league.

(730) Olivia Cooke said after acting in House of the Dragon she is recognised much more in public now - which never happened before despite all the previous shows she was in.

(731) King's Landing often tops polls of fictional places where people would most like to visit.

(732) Some fans think the dragon special effects were better in Game of Thrones than House of the Dragon. It's all subjective.

(733) Paddy Considine was in Hot Fuzz and The World's End -

two films in Edgar Wright's Three Flavours Cornetto trilogy.

(734) Matt Smith said it takes about 90 minutes in makeup to turn him into Daemon Targaryen.

(735) According to an online 'leaker' website, Matt Smith is the highest paid cast member on House of the Dragon.

(736) Olivia Cooke said it felt surreal when she was first told she was going to be in a Game of Thrones prequel.

(737) The Spanish town of Cáceres along with the medieval town of Trujillo were used in scenes for King's Landing in House of the Dragon. Game of Thrones had used Croatia to depict King's Landing.

(738) Prior to House of the Dragon, Ryan Condal was best known for co-creating the sci-fi show Colony.

(739) After the conclusion of the first season of House of the Dragon, it took two years for the second season to arrive.

(740) Paddy Considine said that the illness of Viserys is basically leprosy. Leprosy is a chronic infectious disease caused by the bacterium Mycobacterium leprae. It primarily affects the skin, nerves, and mucous membranes, causing skin lesions, nerve damage, and muscle weakness.

(741) Some of the cast in House of the Dragon have said there aren't that many deleted scenes. Most of what they what shot went into the show.

(742) Rhys Ifans, who plays Ser Otto Hightower, is said to be one of the funniest people on the set and famous for making everyone laugh between takes.

(743) There was a bit of a goof in season one because Paddy Considine was seen wearing a green glove which covered a couple of his fingers. This glove was to aid the CGI used to remove the missing fingers of King Viserys but they obviously forgot to do that. The mistake was quickly rectified by HBO.

(744) Emma D'Arcy said putting on the wigs in House of the Dragon is a great way to get into character.

(745) Game of Thrones star Kit Harington said in 2024 that he'll probably never watch House of the Dragon - at least not for several years.

(746) It was very difficult to keep House of the Dragon's production a secret in 2021 because aerial views showed castle sets at the Leavesden studio backlot.

(747) George RR Martin's books have been described as 'dirty medievalism'. That is to say a fantasy story but one grounded in a medieval realism.

(748) House of the Dragon's drop of viewing figures in season two could be explained by some waiting for it to end so they can binge the episodes later.

(749) The RR in George RR Martin's name stands for Raymond Richard.

(750) Dragons are supposed to be about as intelligent as a dog in George RR Martin's world.

(751) You can buy House of the Dragon tote bags.

(752) In an article for PureWow.com, a 'wig expert' named Brittany Johnson singled out the character Princess Rhaenys

for having one of the worst wigs in the show. Johnson was also none too impressed for the wig used on Matt Smith for when Daemon has short hair.

(753) Rhys Ifans has been in many things but comic book fans might remember him as the Lizard/Dr Curt Connors in The Amazing Spider-Man and Spider-Man: No Way Home.

(754) The origin of dragons is steeped in mythology and folklore from various cultures around the world. They are often depicted as large, serpentine creatures with wings and the ability to breathe fire. In Western mythology, dragons are often seen as malevolent creatures that hoard treasure and terrorize villages. In Eastern mythology, dragons are revered and seen as symbols of power, strength, and good fortune.

(755) Ryan Condal said it was a dream to do House of the Dragon because he was always a big George RR Martin and Game of Thrones nerd.

(756) Paddy Considine was always the first choice to play Viserys.

(757) Cracked.com is another website that has managed to get an article out of the wigs used in House of the Dragon. They complained about Matt Smith being made to look like a knock-off of Legolas from Lord of the Rings.

(758) Jamie Kenna, who plays Ser Alfred Broome, said he thinks that appeal of the Thrones franchise is that it is essentially about dysfunctional families.

(759) George RR Martin had particular praise for Paddy Considine as King Viserys and said he thought that King Viserys was done better in the show than in his book.

(760) Fabien Frankel has made light of the fact that Ser Criston Cole is not exactly the most popular character.

(761) You can buy House of the Dragon phone cases.

(762) House of the Dragon season one has a critic score of 69 on Metacritic. Season two fares slightness better with 73.

(763) Costumes for the show have to be dyed, printed, and decorated.

(764) The Gold Cloaks are - generally - more thuggish and less noble than the White Cloaks.

(765) Tom Glynn-Carney, who plays Aegon Targaryen, said he does yoga to stay in shape during filming.

(766) You can buy House of the Dragon blankets.

(767) HBO have said that going forward they want Game of Thrones spin-off shows to be more diverse in terms of story. They don't just want to constantly do shows about a battle for the Iron Throne.

(768) Jane Goldman, who was the showrunner of the axed spin-off show Bloodmoon, has never spoken about what exactly happened from her point of view. Goldman was said to be 'shocked' when HBO axed the project because she was deep into writing the first season.

(769) Castillo de Coca, a 15th-century brick castle in Spain, was an influence on the designs in House of the Dragon.

(770) To mark season two of House of the Dragon, the Mile End Delicatessen in New York put "Team Green Fire Poutine"

and "Valyrian Cheesecake" on the menu.

(771) The Iron Throne is located in the Great Hall of the Red Keep.

(772) George RR Martin is not really much of a social media user and prefers to communicate through blog posts.

(773) Milly Alcock was cast before Emily Carey.

(774) Viserys wears the chain of office which was worn by his grandfather King Jaehaerys.

(775) Eve Best said that she was vague about the fate of Rhaenys because she didn't read the book and avoid reading all the season two scripts in advance. She said she did have an inkling about what might happen though because her contract was only for two seasons.

(776) You can buy House of the Dragon themed coasters online.

(777) The world of Westeros is known for its intricate and detailed world-building, including rich histories, diverse cultures, and dynamic political landscapes.

(778) Caroline McCall, who took over as the lead costume designer in season two, had not yet watched the first season of House of the Dragon when she was hired.

(779) Emily Carey said it was 'bitterweet' to leave House of the Dragon so that another actor could take over the part.

(780) Olivia Cooke is known as 'Liv' to her friends.

(781) Papa John's released a 'Dragon Flame' pizza in Florida in 2022 to celebrate House of the Dragon.

(782) The Iron Throne is sharp enough to cut anyone who isn't careful. It is said that if someone is cut by the Iron Throne they are doomed.

(783) Targaryens - famously - are prone to madness on occasion.

(784) HBO put out 'duelling' trailers for season two. One was for Team Black and the other for Team Green.

(785) The dragon riders in House of the Dragon (sensibly) have saddles.

(786) You can buy House of the Dragon stationary.

(787) The riot sequence in episode six of season two required 300 extras.

(788) Matt Smith described his character Daemon as 'an agent of chaos'.

(789) You can buy a House of the Dragon colouring book online.

(790) Season one of House of the Dragon was released on 4K with 70 minutes of extras.

(791) Emma D'Arcy's background is mostly theatre. It was Emma's performances on the stage which attracted the attention of House of the Dragon's casting director.

(792) Bourne Wood, which has been used in many productions

including House of the Dragon, is popular for period films and TV shows because it has large clearings and no telephone pylons in the background.

(793) The dragons in George RR Martin's fictional universe are exceptionally powerful due to their ability to breathe fire. They are mighty weapons of mass destruction.

(794) The Hightower sigil depicts a white tower with flames on smoke gray.

(795) Danny Sapani was considered for the part of Corlys Velaryon.

(796) Emily Carey said there were a lot of nerves on the set when House of the Dragon started shooting. Everyone knew this show had big shoes to fill.

(797) The Iron Throne was implanted in the Tower of London to promote House of the Dragon in 2022.

(798) Gray's Papaya in New York did a 'Dragonstone Dog' to mark season two. The hot dog was topped with jalapeños.

(799) You can buy a House of the Dragon lunch box.

(800) Olivia Cooke said that House of the Dragon was perfect timing for her because she'd just moved back to England after living in the United States for a while. House of the Dragon is made at a studio near London so it meant Olivia could go home and sleep in her own bed!

(801) The Targaryen dynasty was obviously built on the back of dragons. Having dragons gave them a huge military advantage over rivals.

(802) The construction of the Red Keep was completed by Maegor I, aka Maegor the Cruel.

(803) Graham McTavish, who appears in House of the Dragon as Ser Harrold Westerling, said he was offered his pick of two different parts in the show. He declined the other part because the character was killed off early!

(804) Emma D'Arcy said she felt a bit lonely shooting season two of House of the Dragon because she didn't see much of Matt Smith and Olivia Cooke.

(805) Dragons often couldn't fly in medieval literature.

(806) You can buy Targaryen Sigil Christmas ornaments.

(807) John's of Bleeker Street created a special pizza to celebrate season two. The pizza features green peppers to represent 'Team Green'.

(808) The design of the dragons in the show begins with 3-D models.

(809) You can buy a Rhaenyra Targaryen Dress Costume online.

(810) Eve Best said she asked for Princess Rhaenys Velaryon to have a whip and this wish was granted. She was even given whip lessons!

(811) Emily Carey said that away from acting she likes to relax by playing with LEGO!

(812) The costume department on House of the Dragon employs textile artists, embroiderers, metal workers, and

leather workers.

(813) HBO put the first episode of House of the Dragon free on YouTube to give people a taste of the show.

(814) There is a House of the Dragon official podcast - in addition to a number of unofficial ones too.

(815) Graham McTavish, who appears in House of the Dragon as Ser Harrold Westerling, is no stranger to fantasy because he was in the three Hobbit films.

(816) The first season title sequence takes place over a 3D stone model of Old Valyria.

(817) The costume designer said that Rhaenyra's jewelry in season one was partly inspired by traditional Moroccan brides.

(818) Fire and Blood explores themes of destiny, sacrifice, and legacy. As the Targaryen family grapples with questions of fate and duty, we see how their choices reverberate through the generations.

(819) Harry Collett, who plays Jacaerys Velaryon, said he did three taped auditions and then went to the studio for a more formal audition.

(820) Graham McTavish was once in a Rambo film with Sly Stallone. The film he was in was the fourth entry in the Rambo franchise.

(821) The big 'battle' between House of the Dragon and Rings of Power was sometimes dubbed Dragons v Elves in the media.

(822) You can buy House of the Dragon calenders.

(823) Matt Smith said while riding the 'bucking bronco' for the dragon riding scenes aren't much fun he simply reminds himself there are people out there with far worse jobs!

(824) Paddy Considine said that the makeup to depict the disfigured King Viserys was a bit of a pain because he had to spend hours in the makeup chair.

(825) You can buy a House of the Dragon King's Hand pin badge on Etsy.

(826) A line of House of the Dragon action figures are now available to pre-order.

(827) Milly Alcock abandoned acting school in Australia to take a role in House of the Dragon.

(828) Ryan Condal likened the skirmish between Vhagar and Arrax to a rhino taking on a cat.

(829) Some critics felt the structure of season two of House of the Dragon was somewhat baffling in that the big battle came at the midway point and then the rest of the season was what you could describe as low-key or slow burn. The structure of Game of Thrones was to have a huge penultimate episode followed by an eventful 'aftermath' finale.

(830) Dragonmont is a volcanic peak rife with tunnels and caverns.

(831) There was some House of the Dragon content in Game of Thrones: Conquest. Game of Thrones: Conquest is a free-to-play strategy game.

(832) Miguel Sapochnik suggested some of the names of characters should be changed in House of the Dragon because they were too similar (for example, Princess Rhaenyra and Princess Rhaenys) but Ryan Condal refused to do this because he wanted to be faithful to George RR Martin's character names.

(833) It is said that HBO were initially dubious about turning Game of Thrones into a franchise because they suspected Thrones was a one-off sensation that could never be replicated.

(834) Ryan Condal said that the older Princess Rhaenyra was the most difficult part to cast in the show.

(835) There are apparently some animated Game of Thrones spin-off shows in the works at HBO.

(836) Paddy Considine was in the acclaimed show Peaky Blinders.

(837) George RR Martin said he didn't like the way the media depicted House of the Dragon and Rings of Power as being in competition with each other. George said he thought that was a bit silly.

(838) Out of the first two seasons, The Hollywood Reporter ranked The Lord of the Tides as the best episode.

(839) Out of the first two seasons, The Hollywood Reporter ranked The Queen Who Ever Was as the worst episode.

(840) You can buy a House of the Dragon wallet online.

(841) Casting director Kate Rhodes James said she got the idea

to cast Tom Glynn-Carney as Prince Aegon after watching him in a play called The Ferryman.

(842) Ryan Condal said his first instinct was that HBO should do a Dunk & Egg show as the first Game of Thrones spin-off but he said that both HBO and George RR Martin were much more enthusiastic about doing what became House of the Dragon.

(843) The cast on House of the Dragon are often buffeted by wind machines when they shoot a scene where a dragon is near them.

(844) Olivia Cooke said she doesn't like Instagram very much but considers it a necessary burden in terms of her career.

(845) There was 20 weeks of pre-production on season two.

(846) There is a bigger female presence on House of the Dragon when it comes to writers and directors than there was on Game of Thrones.

(847) Season two of House of the Dragon has a mediocre rating of 6.5 on IMDB.

(848) An extra on Game of Thrones would usually get paid about £100 a day. We can presume there is a similar sort of payment on House of the Dragon.

(849) The television universe based on George Rr Martin's books was nearly over before it began. The original pilot episode for Game of Thrones was so bad that HBO considered scrapping the entire project. Thankfully they didn't do that. They reshot the pilot and went ahead.

(850) Millie Alcock said that when she watches House of the Dragon now she sort of forgets she was once in the show! Richard Madden said much the same thing when he left Game of Thrones.

(851) The cast of House of the Dragon had a slightly easier time than the cast of Game of Thrones because the production base in southern England is a bit warmer and less wet than Northern Ireland.

(852) Olivia Cooke said she avoided reading anything about House of the Dragon online and on social media until some of the episodes had come out.

(853) HBO initially rejected the idea of doing a Dunk & Egg spin-off show but they obviously changed their mind about that in the end.

(854) You can buy House of the Dragon Beanie Hats.

(855) It is probably fair to say that most fans felt season two of House of the Dragon was weaker and more underwhelming than season one.

(856) An article in Soapcentral.com ranked Alicent Hightower as the most 'hated' character.

(857) HBO considered fifteen different spin-off ideas and pitches before deciding on House of the Dragon.

(858) Matt Smith said it is very hard to remember the names of the dragons in the show!

(859) Ryan Condal described Silverwing as the 'Concorde' of dragons.

(860) The production team on House of the Dragon spent many weeks designing the specific look of each dragon in the show.

(861) Ser Gerold Royce does not appear in the books and is a character created for the television show.

(862) Ryan Condal had to relocate to England to make House of the Dragon.

(863) When he did his first House of the Dragons panel at Comic-Con, Matt Smith was delighted to run into his friend and former Doctor Who co-star Karen Gillan. Karen was doing a Marvel panel because of her role in the Guardians of the Galaxy franchise.

(864) In the scene with Viserys and Daemon where the king'a crown falls off and Daemon picks it up, this was a complete accident that they decided to leave in because it made for a poignant moment.

(865) House of the Dragon, like most modern shows, employs intimacy coordinators.

(866) Milly Alcock said that when she was cast in House of the dragon she was only given two scripts initially because the others were being rewritten.

(867) Critics of House of the Dragon have complained that the show's second season basically kept the characters in a repeating loop that went nowhere. It was 'table setting' rather than action. Of course this is all purely subjective and down to individual opinion.

(868) The jousting tournament at the start of House of the

Dragon is called the Heirs Tournament.

(869) Paddy Considine said the Red Keep set was the most amazing set he has ever encountered in his acting career.

(870) You can buy a Targaryen Sigil Ring online.

(871) Graham McTavish was photographed on the set of House of the Dragon early into production. Fans were even able to guess which character he would playing (despite the fact that information hadn't been revealed yet).

(872) Season one of House of the Dragon had to halt production a couple of times due to positive covid tests.

(873) Harry Collett, who plays Jacaerys Velaryon, is one of the few actors in the show who doesn't wear a wig. He simply grew his hair long.

(874) Jefferson Hall, who plays the Lannister twins, has joked that the House of the Dragon producers must have forgot he had a small part in Game of Thrones!

(875) In the Chinese zodiac, the dragon is one of the twelve animal signs and is believed to bring luck, strength, and success.

(876) The chains worn by Otto Hightower were handcrafted for the show.

(877) Hunter Schafer was considered for the part of Rhaenyra.

(878) Graham McTavish has done voice acting for the Uncharted and Call of Duty video game franchises.

(879) Tom Glynn-Carney said he tried to make King Aegon II complex and not just a pure villain.

(880) You can buy Targaryen themed underwear on Etsy.

(881) HBO created an AR App to promote House of the Dragon.

(882) At the time of writing Smallfolk is the lowest rated episode of House of the Dragon on IMDB with 6.2 out of ten.

(883) The set designers on House of the Dragon said they try to avoid drapes in the Red Keep because it makes everything seem a bit Victorian.

(884) A writer for The Ringer once had an article saying he struggles with House of the Dragon because he doesn't like watching the scenes where the dragons perish or get hurt.

(885) Emily Carey said that House of the Dragon was the first acting job she ever had where she was now old enough not to need a chaperone on the set.

(886) George RR Martin did a blog post in July 2024 in which he said he would not be attending the forthcoming writer's meeting for season three of House of the Dragon. Some interpreted this as George implying that he'd either been elbowed out of the show by HBO or had simply decided to wash his hands of it after being unhappy with the changes made from the book. This is purely speculation though.

(887) In a 2022 article, the Guardian newspaper dubbed House of the Dragon as 'Game of Groans' and complained that the show was boring.

(888) The dragon battle scenes in House of the Dragon took

some inspiration from World War II 'dog fights' in the air.

(889) Targaryan red crest banners were draped on the Rockefeller Center to promote season two.

(890) Dark Sister is one of the ancestral Valyrian blades of House Targaryen.

(891) Once it has bonded with someone, a dragon will not let anyone else ride it.

(892) Some were surprised that Paddy Considine didn't get any major nominations for his performance in season one.

(893) You can buy a House of the Dragon 'dragon egg light'.

(894) George RR Martin's books have a very obvious anti-war message. The wars in his books are brutal and often senseless.

(896) Before it came out out, there was some speculation that House of the Dragon would be narrated and framed by Bran (from Game of Thrones) but this obviously didn't happen in the end.

(897) The Targaryen sigil is a red three-headed dragon.

(898) Ryan Condal said they changed the title sequence for season two because they wanted something that would be constantly altered to reflect what was happening in the story. They also thought it would be more visually interesting for the audience.

(899) The Iron Throne was created after Aegon I Targaryen was victorious and left with a huge collection of vanquished enemy swords.

(900) Olivia Cooke said the reason she'd never watched Game of Thrones until she was cast in a prequel is that she is suspicious of things which are really popular. Olivia said she was wrong to have this attitude though because Game of Thrones turned out to be really good.

(901) Vhager is known as the Queen of Dragons.

(902) After the completion of the Red Keep, Maegor I Targaryen had all the builders killed so that the secrets and passageways would remain a secret.

(903) Graham McTavish said he turned down a part in Game of Thrones some years ago. Graham did not say which part it was.

(904) Paddy Considine has a Funko Pop! figure of Viserys Targaryen in his office.

(905) Alicent is also more sympathetic in the show than in the book. There has been some criticism (not from everyone naturally) that House of the Dragon tends to try and make the two female characters 'nicer' than their literary counterparts.

(906) Milly Alcock and Emily Carey were given half as a season as the young Rhaenyra and Alicent because Ryan Condal didn't want them to be a mere flashback or prologue.

(907) You can buy House of the Dragon socks.

(908) Matt Smith said the wigs in the show are a bit of a pain at times because you have to have them fitted each time you come in for shooting.

(909) Prince Aemond Targaryen is sometimes known as

"Aemond One-Eye".

(910) Mashable named The Lord of the Tides as the third best television episode of 2022.

(911) When season two came out, a bagel shop in New York put a 'bacon, Aegon and cheese' bagel on the menu.

(912) Targaryen banners were draped at Citi Field to promote season two. Citi Field is the home of the New York Mets.

(913) The 80th floor of the Empire State Building was transformed into an immersive House of the Dragon experience to promote season two.

(914) The immersive experience at the Empire State Building gave guests (what else?) dragon fruit sorbet which came with its own dragon toy figure.

(915) The logos and promotional imagery of House of the Dragon are deliberately similar to Game of Thrones for obvious commercial reasons.

(916) When the first ever episode of House of the Dragon came out, 1.3 million people in Britain stayed up to watch the premiere at 2am.

(917) Paddy Considine said the film he supposed to do after House of the Dragon fell through so he was basically unemployed for a while once his time on the show ended!

(918) In a poll on the German version of YouGov in 2022, a surprisingly high 52% of respondents said they had no interest in watching House of the Dragon.

(919) House of the Dragon production designer Jim Clay said he tried to push away slightly from a European medieval sensibility and take in some Roman and Byzantine influences.

(920) As far as the 'duel' with Rings of Power went, House of Dragon seemed to be a fairly clear victor in 2022. According to streaming figures, only 37% of people who started watching Rings of Power went on to finish the first season.

(921) Larys Strong has a firefly symbol on his cane. This is a personal symbol and not the sigil of House Strong.

(922) You can buy a Daemon Targaryen Cosplay Costume online.

(923) Ramin Djawadi said the reason why Game of Thrones and House of the Dragon share the same theme music is that they wanted the two shows to feel like blood relatives.

(924) Prince Aemond Targaryen has a blue sapphire under his eye-patch.

(925) You can buy a cosplay version of the green dress that Alicent Hightower wears.

(926) Eve Best, who played Princess Rhaenys Velaryon in House of the Dragon, said her audition involved doing a scene from Game of Thrones with the character names changed.

(927) You can buy a House of the Dragon goblet which changes colour.

(928) Aegon Targaryen is supposed to be eighteen at the start of season two. Tom Glynn-Carney was actually 29 in real life though.

(929) Emily Carey said that House of the Dragon was the best of both worlds for her in that she got a career boost without being tied down to something for several years.

(930) GQ once had an article which opined that the characters in House of the Dragon were bungling and not very bright compared to the likes of Tywin, Varys, and Littlefinger in Game of Thrones.

(931) The second season finale of House of the Dragon has a mediocre 6.3 rating on IMDB.

(932) Bars have done a number of House of the Dragon themed cocktails to celebrate the show.

(933) Graham McTavish said his acting dream would be to play a James Bond villain.

(934) Tom Glynn-Carney said he binged all eight seasons of Game of Thrones in three weeks when he was cast in House of the Dragon. He'd never watched Game of Thrones before.

(935) House of the Dragon partnered with Merrell to create a line of sneakers. The three different shoe lines are called Targaryen, Velaryon, and Hightower.

(936) Phia Saban, who plays Helaena Targaryen, also tested to play the younger version of Rhaenyra.

(937) In an interview, Ryan Condal seemed to suggest that George RR Martin didn't have any creative participation in season two of House of the Dragon.

(938) George RR Martin did a blog post in 2024 lambasting television and film writers for changing the novels they are

adapting too much. Though he cited no examples some wondered if his subtext was about season two of House of the Dragon. This is purely speculation though.

(939) Milly Alcock appeared in the music video for the song "Easy Now" by Noel Gallagher's High Flying Birds.

(940) Michele Carragher was the principal embroidery artist on Game of Thrones and House of the Dragon.

(941) The Targaryen dynasty was a mixture of greatness and tragedy.

(942) A writer on the NY Post once wrote an article saying he struggled with House of the Dragon because he could never remember the names of all the different characters! To be fair, it does help if you are familiar with the book.

(943) Jousting was a popular and iconic medieval sport that involved mounted knights charging at each other with lances in hand. Jousting originated as a military exercise to train knights for combat. It evolved into a sport and spectacle in medieval Europe.

(944) The first teaser trailer for House of the Dragon got ten million views in one day.

(945) Feasting was a common practice in medieval society, with elaborate banquets held for special occasions and celebrations.

(946) Steve Toussaint's first screen acting credit was a small part in an episode of the beloved Sherlock Holmes television series with Jeremy Brett.

(947) Jousting tournaments were popular forms of entertainment for medieval audiences, often accompanied by feasting, music, and other festivities.

(948) You might recall previously seeing Jefferson Hall in the 2018 film Halloween. He played a true crime podcaster trying to track down Laurie Strode.

(949) Graham McTavish has released his own brand of bourbon whiskey. The beverage is called The Warchief.

(950) In jousting, points were awarded for breaking a lance on an opponent's armor or pushing them off their horse.

(951) Harry Collett, who plays Jacaerys Velaryon, said that on his initial auditions he had no idea this was a Game of Thrones prequel. It was all top secret.

(952) Jefferson Hall said he read Fire & Blood to prepare for House of the Dragon.

(953) Jousting tournaments were usually sponsored by wealthy nobles or royalty, who provided prizes and rewards for the victors.

(954) In the book, King Viserys was 29 when he married Alicent. Paddy Considine was 48 though when Viserys and Alicent get together in the show.

(955) House of the Dragon is slightly atypical in the modern era because it isn't all (in Netflix style) dropped in one block to binge in its entirety.

(956) When he played the Doctor in Doctor Who, Matt Smith was once in an episode titled Cold War which had Game of

Thrones actors Liam Cunningham and Tobias Menzies in the cast.

(957) You can buy a House Targaryen drinking tankard online.

(958) You can buy the first two seasons of House of the Dragon on Blu-Ray.

(959) George RR Martin said that originally he wasn't going to have any dragons in his books but in the end he couldn't resist it.

(960) Eve Best brought some champagne for the cast and crew on her last ever day on House of the Dragon.

(961) One obvious problem with adapting Fire & Blood is that there are accounts of mighty battles and it is almost impossible for a television show to have an expensive battle in every other episode.

(962) The Crabfeeder wears a mask because he has Greyscale.

(963) Emilia Clarke said in 2024 that she has no idea what House of the Dragon is about and will never watch it. She did say though that she wished everyone on the show all the best and hoped it did well.

(964) Paddy Considine said that the makeup to depict the disfigured King Viserys did feel quite constrictive.

(965) 5,000 costumes were created for the extras to wear in season two of House of the Dragon.

(966) Ryan Condal said it was Matt Smith's work on The Crown rather than Doctor Who which made them think of

him for House of the Dragon.

(967) Tom Bennett, who plays plays Ulf the White, said he ended up eating 30 quails shooting a feast scene in the season two finale.

(968) Rhys Ifans is apparently the wealthiest House of the Dragon cast member. He has a reported net wealth of $12 million.

(969) King Viserys I Targaryen is remembered as Viserys The Peaceful.

(970) The second season of House of the Dragon got a limited edition 4K Steelbox release.

(971) Ryan Condal said that the big dragon sequence in the first season finale was like a sort of test run for the production team. They knew if they could make this sequence work it would give them valuable experience and knowledge when it came to pulling off the bigger dragon battles to come.

(972) When a character is close to a dragon in the show they have a giant dragon's head operated by puppeteers for the actor to interact with. Special effects are obviously used later to put the dragon in through CGI.

(973) House of the Dragon was actually the first spin-off show that HBO had ever done.

(974) Among the spin-off pitches that HBO considered (before deciding on House of the Dragon) was one about the fall of the ancient Targaryen empire of Valyria.

(975) Another spin-off pitch HBO rejected was one about

Aegon's conquest of Westeros.

(976) A spin-off show about the Dornish warrior queen Nymeria was also rejected by HBO before they did House of the Dragon.

(977) Jefferson Hall went to the same acting school as Kit Harington. They were a year apart.

(978) George RR Martin said he has never seen the Bloodmoon pilot. It seems the pilot is locked in a HBO vault somewhere and they don't want anyone to watch it.

(979) Olivia Cooke said that Cersei was her favourite character in Game of Thrones.

(980) George RR Martin said, when it comes to the television shows based on his books, he would hate to end up like a sort of mascot with no creative control or influence over the content going into production.

(981) Sara Hess, who is executive producer and a writer on House of the Dragon, said she has never watched Game of Thrones.

(982) Movieweb.com ranked Alicent Hightower as the best character in season one.

(983) Some fans felt the Driftmark set was overused in season two.

(984) You can buy a House of the Dragon cat collar.

(985) Casting director Kate Rhodes James said they never discussed any other actor apart from Matt Smith for the part

of Daemon.

(986) Ryan Condal has defended the 'slow burn' nature of House of the Dragon. His view is that you need to spend time with these characters before they all start fighting each other.

(987) Olivia Cooke got her first acting break playing Christopher Eccleston's daughter in a BBC drama called Blackout. Eccleston, like Matt Smith, has played the Doctor in Doctor Who.

(988) The set decorators on House of the Dragon unavoidably spend a lot of time arranging candles.

(989) Milly Alcock beat Emilia Jones and Meg Donnelly to get the part of Supergirl.

(990) James Gunn said it was House of the Dragon which made him aware of Milly Alcock and decide to cast her as Supergirl.

(991) The Valyrian language has different dialects to make it feel more realistic.

(992) Though you wouldn't know it from his music scores, Ramin Djawadi said he is a fan of heavy metal music in real life!

(993) George RR Martin said he didn't like the hunting scene leading to King Robert's death in Game of Thrones because there were so few extras and characters as part of the hunt. He was much happier with the hunting scene in season one of House of the Dragon.

(994) According to Mediacsuite.com, House of the Dragon is the seventh most expensive television show of all time. In

case you were wondering, the only shows more expensive to make were The Pacific, Stranger Things, Rings of Power, and some of the Marvel shows.

(995) Game of Thrones became a cultural phenomenon, with fans around the world hosting viewing parties. House of the Dragon hasn't really grabbed casual viewers in the same way and attracted that sort of excitement and devotion but then Thrones is an impossible act to follow.

(996) A poll for Boston.com voted Daemon Targaryen as the best character in House of the Dragon with 42% of the vote.

(997) House of the Dragon was the most pirated show of 2022 - accounting for 17% of all illegal streams and torrents when it came to TV shows.

(998) You can buy a King Viserys Targaryen soy candle. The dominant scent is blackberry.

(999) The dragon Vermithor is known as the Bronze Fury.

(1000) Some of the actors in House of the Dragon said it was titled 'Red Gun' when they did their audition to disguise the fact it was a Thrones spin-off.

## Photo Credit

https://pixabay.com/illustrations/ai-generated-dragon-wood-dragon-8578276/


18 February 2024

artieblur